USAF WARRIOR STUDIES

Richard H. Kohn and Joseph P. Harahan
General Editors

The original edition of this work was published as a Special Study—RESTRICTED—by Headquarters, Army Air Forces, Office of the Assistant Chief of Air Staff, Washington, D.C., in March 1946. The study was approved by Headquarters, United States Air Forces in Europe and Headquarters, Army Air Forces. All the information in the original edition, including the title and subtitle, appears in its entirety in this reprint.

Copies of the original edition may be consulted at the USAF Air University Library, Maxwell Air Force Base, Alabama, or the US Army Military History Institute, Carlisle Barracks, Pennsylvania.

Special Study • ~~RESTRICT~~ *March 1946*

Condensed Analysis of the

Ninth Air Force

in the European Theater of Operations

An analytical study of the operating procedures and functional organization of tactical air power as developed by the NINTH AIR FORCE in the war of Western Europe

APPROVED BY HEADQUARTERS, UNITED STATES AIR FORCES IN EUROPE
HEADQUARTERS, ARMY AIR FORCES

★

HEADQUARTERS, ARMY AIR FORCES
OFFICE OF ASSISTANT CHIEF OF AIR STAFF
WASHINGTON, D. C.

THE EDITORS OF THIS STUDY wish to express their apprec tion to the Headquarters, Army Air Forces, for its assistance final preparation and publication; to the Commanding General, Unit States Air Forces in Europe, and his immediate staff for their thorou review of the study and constructive suggestions for revision to ensu the soundness of conclusions and recommendations; and to the Co manding Generals and their staffs of the Ninth Air Force and its co mands for their unstinted cooperation in making all types information available and their energetic efforts to make the study complete and thorough as possible.

This publication was prepared and edited by Col. William B. Re Executive Chief of Staff, Ninth Air Force. He was assisted by Lt. C Thomas C. Quinlan, Lt. Col. Chester K. Shore, Capt. Ellwood E. Ge sler, and Capt. Robert S. Gerdy.

A limited number of additional copies of this publication may be secured by addressing requests to Commanding General, Army Air Forces, Washington 25, D. C., Publication Division, Air Adjutant General.

TABLE OF CONTENTS

v

hapter V.—Conclusions and Recommendations: Internal—Continued

CONDENSED ANALYSIS OF THE
NINTH AIR FORCE

IN THE EUROPEAN THEATER
OF OPERATIONS

An analytical study of the
operating procedures and
functional organization of
tactical air power as developed
by the Ninth Air Force in the
war of Western Europe

New Imprint by
OFFICE OF AIR FORCE HISTORY
UNITED STATES AIR FORCE
WASHINGTON, D.C., 1984

Library of Congress Cataloging in Publication Data
Main entry under title:

Condensed analysis of the Ninth Air Force in the European theater of operations.

(USAF warrior studies)
Reprint. Originally published: Washington, D.C.: Headquarters, Army Air Forces, Office of Assistant Chief of Air Staff, 1946. (Special study)
1. World War, 1939–1945—Aerial operations, American. 2. United States. Army Air Forces. Air Force, 9th—Organization. 3. United States. Army Air Forces—Tactical aviation. 4. Air warfare. I. Reed, William B. II. United States. Air Force. Office of Air Force History III. Series.
D790.C655 1984 940.54'4973 84-2352
ISBN 0-912799-13-7

Project Warrior Studies are published by the Office of Air Force History. The views expressed in this book were those of the United States Army Air Forces in 1946 and do not necessarily reflect the official views and policies of the United States Air Force and the Department of Defense today.

For sale by the Superintendent of Documents, U.S. Government Printing Office
Washington, D.C. 20402

FOREWORD

The publication of the *Condensed Analysis of the Ninth Air Force in the European Theater of Operations* is part of a continuing series of historical studies from the Office of Air Force History in support of Project Warrior.

Project Warrior seeks to create and maintain within the Air Force an environment where Air Force people at all levels can learn from the past and apply the warfighting experiences of past generations to the present. When Gen. Lew Allen, Jr., initiated the project in 1982, he called for the "continuing study of military history, combat leadership, the principles of war and, particularly, the applications of air power." All of us in the Air Force community can benefit from such study and reflection. The challenges of today and the future demand no less.

CHARLES A. GABRIEL, General, USAF
Chief of Staff

PREFACE

In an effort to help Air Force people better understand how the United States organizes, trains, equips, sustains and employs aerospace forces for theater air operations, the Office of Air Force History, in support of Project Warrior, has undertaken to reprint two important historical documents. The first is the 1943 "Magna Carta" of an independent air force, War Department Field Manual 100–20, *Command and Employment of Air Power,* published last year as an appendix to the Warrior study, *Air Superiority in World War II and Korea.* The second, reprinted here, is the *Condensed Analysis of Ninth Air Force Operations in the European Theater of Operations.*

The *Condensed Analysis* contains a short history of the Ninth Air Force in World War II, from the build-up before the invasion of the European continent through subsequent combat operations in 1944 and 1945. More than a narrative history, the study examines the problems that Ninth experienced in conducting joint combat operations with ground forces across the rapidly moving battlefront in France and Germany. Some of its recommendations were implemented after World War II, others involve issues we continue to struggle with today: The need for a theater level air headquarters, command and control of tactical air forces, the importance of air-ground cooperation (including the co-location of headquarters), and the absence of the capability to mount night and all-weather operations—the lack of a "real and effective 24-hour-a-day operation." In its comprehensiveness, the *Condensed Analysis* also touches aircrew training and rotation, air base defense organization, civil engineering support, intelligence—virtually every one of today's Air Force specialities.

Since 1945 the Air Force has gone far in creating a modernized force structure with highly professional personnel. Yet many of the doctrinal problems identified during World War II are still with us today. A look back, therefore, can be a useful reminder of how such problems developed and how they might be solved.

JOHN T. CHAIN
Lieutenant General, USAF
Deputy Chief of Staff, Plans and Operations

FOREWORD

TO THE 1946 EDITION

IT HAS BECOME axiomatic that air superiority, tactical and strategic, is essential to success in modern total war. In western Europe tactical air power was a dominating and decisive factor which contributed largely to the neutralization of enemy air power, the disruption of enemy channels of communication and the destruction of enemy troops and matériel in closest cooperation with the ground forces.

Tactical air power, however, did not reach full maturity in the war in western Europe. The tactical air forces never ceased to experiment, to sharpen their sensitivity to changes in the ground situation or to increase the timeliness and destructiveness of their operations. The complexity of this effort may be seen in the fact that the Ninth Air Force's area of responsibility extended over the front and rear of all enemy forces facing the Ninth, First and Third U. S. Armies and that—within this huge area—every military installation, whether air, ground, naval, supply, or vital industry, was a possible and often an essential target.

This study attempts to show why the Ninth Air Force had to reach an unusual degree of flexibility and mobility in 19 months of operation from six different European countries and will show that the effort to achieve these two characteristics was at the root of almost every organizational and procedural change in the air force.

In applying against the enemy the largest force of tactical aircraft ever assembled under one command, the officers and men of the Ninth Air Force gained invaluable experience in organizing and reorganizing functionally the many units of a tactical air force in accordance with the current operating procedures developed in a rapidly changing, intricate war. The task of organizing the air force initially and then modifying its organization constantly in accord with new tactical requirements was made more difficult by the fact that there were no precise models to follow, no conventional structure to imitate. Consequently it will be seen in the study that the development of the Ninth Air Force was characterized by departure from conventional laws of growth.

This report, which attempts to analyze briefly the organizational and operational evolution of the Ninth Air Force and to present certain general conclusions, which were reached by its commanders and their staffs, must be considered as a pioneer effort, presented factually but subject to change. No greater or more dangerous mistake could be made than to assume that the same policies and procedures which won the tactical air war in Europe would necessarily have been appropriate in the Philippines, China, Africa, or any other part of the world. However, the experience of the Ninth Air Force in Europe can certainly be used as a guide which will help suggest answers to tactical air problems and, further, should be of general interest to all students of tactical air warfare.

Perhaps the basic conclusion of this study—the principle which Ninth Air Force commanders agreed was the secret of the air force's success in combat—is that *flexibility and mobility in thought, policy and action are vitally essential to the successful prosecution of a tactical air war.*

This condensed study precedes a larger, more detailed report on the operating procedures and functional organization of the Ninth Air Force. Both works have been prepared in the conviction that this material will be of immediate and active interest to planners, organizers and students of tactical air power.

HOYT S. VANDENBERG
Lieutenant General, U. S. A.

ACKNOWLEDGMENTS

1946 EDITION

THE EDITORS OF THIS STUDY wish to express their appreciation to the Headquarters, Army Air Forces, for its assistance in final preparation and publication; to the Commanding General, United States Air Forces in Europe, and his immediate staff for their thorough review of the study and constructive suggestions for revision to ensure the soundness of conclusions and recommendations; and to the Commanding Generals and their staffs of the Ninth Air Force and its commands for their unstinted cooperation in making all types of information available and their energetic efforts to make the study as complete and thorough as possible.

This publication was prepared and edited by Col. William B. Reed, Executive Chief of Staff, Ninth Air Force. He was assisted by Lt. Col. Thomas C. Quinlan, Lt. Col. Chester K. Shore, Capt. Ellwood E. Geissler, and Capt. Robert S. Gerdy.

United States Air Force Historical Advisory Committee

(As of April 1, 1984)

Lt. Gen. Charles G. Cleveland, USAF
Commander, Air University

Mr. DeWitt S. Copp
The National Volunteer Agency

Dr. Philip A. Crowl
Annapolis, Maryland

Dr. Warren W. Hassler, Jr.
Pennsylvania State University

Brig. Gen. Harris B. Hull, USAF, Retired
National Aeronautics and Space Administration

Dr. Alfred F. Hurley
Brig. Gen., USAF, Retired
North Texas State University

Gen. Bryce Poe II, USAF, Retired
Alexandria, Virginia

Lt. Gen. Winfield W. Scott, Jr., USAF
Superintendent, USAF Academy

Dr. David A. Shannon (*Chairman*)
University of Virginia

Mr. Eugene R. Sullivan
The General Counsel, USAF

TABLE OF CONTENTS

Chapter V.—Conclusions and Recommendations: Internal—Continued

MAPS

Facing page 48

CHARTS

Chapter I

INTRODUCTION

THE MISSION of a tactical air force as defined and outlined in Field Manual 100–20, "Command and Employment of Air Power," proved entirely sound throughout the operations of the Ninth Air Force in the European theater. The division of the mission into three separate inter-related phases and the priority assigned to each phase are unassailable.

In the campaign in western Europe, where the precision team-work of the Allied air, ground and naval forces accomplished battle miracles, the basic military conception that air, land and sea power are co-equal and inter-dependent was confirmed beyond all reasonable doubt. Interdependence being both strategic and tactical, any arrangement of our armed forces which might prejudice the equality of the three arms would similarly prejudice our success in war.

The Field Commander of the 12th Army Group, Gen. Omar N. Bradley, might well have had this principle in mind when he made the following statement at Wiesbaden, Germany, on 15 July 1945: "The axiomatic requirement that victory can only be achieved by the attainment of supremacy on the land, sea and in the air has never been so fully proven as in this total defeat of an enemy who never controlled the sea, who tried to substitute strategic artillery for a defeat in the air, and whose armed forces were crushed and homeland over-run by the combined power of our supremacy in all these three elements."

Tactical air power participated as a full partner of the Army and the Navy in the diversified operations of the three arms against Germany. It coordinated its efforts directly with the armies in all phases of the ground battle, with the Navy in certain minor sea skirmishes and in attacks on shipping, harbors, docks, inland waterways, and other naval installations, and with both in the assault by the invasion armada upon the Normandy beaches. Tactical air power provided visual reconnaissance and aerial photography for all services, aided in the movement of troops and critical supplies and attacked and seriously disrupted or severed the enemy's vital communications behind the battle lines.

By far the largest tactical air component in the European Theater of

Operations was the Ninth Air Force, which was officially reconstituted in the United Kingdom on 16 October 1943. Less than eight months later, in May 1944, this air force had reached almost full stature and was powerful enough to furnish an impenetrable shield of air might over the greatest single military undertaking of the war—the invasion of western Europe. The activation, organization, equipping, training and introduction into combat of the several hundreds of tactical, administrative, service, and technical units comprising this enormous air striking force in such a remarkably short period of time represents one of the outstanding organizational and operational achievements in the history of aviation.

The tactical air war in Europe was marked by continuous development which was still going on vigorously after VE-day, 7 May 1945. This study, however, covers only the actual period of organization and operations. As General Vandenberg points out in the foreword, the development of the functional organization and operating procedure of the Ninth Air Force was extraordinarily rapid and considerably different from that of conventional air force organizations. This necessitated a continuing review of its functions and procedures, with the basic principle always in mind that the highest standards of flexibility and mobility had to be maintained.

Flexibility in organization, policy, thought and action is a prime prerequisite to success in tactical air war. An unusual degree of organizational and operational flexibility enabled the Ninth Air Force promptly to apply its total tactical power, or any required portion of it, where it could damage the enemy most materially and permit the ground forces most fully to exploit the enemy's diminishing power to resist. This flexibility also enabled the air force to achieve maximum effectiveness in coordinated efforts with other air forces and with the army group. It permitted the diversion of tactical air power, rapidly to meet critical situations on the ground, to nullify sudden enemy air opposition or, generally, to shift from one phase of operations to another, thereby frequently making it possible for individual ground force units to face superior strength in armor, firepower and troops.

The evolution of staff organization and procedures in air force and command headquarters reflected the commander's determination to maintain the highest degree of flexibility in his organization. Frequently the appearance of new responsibilities made it necessary for the air force to create new parts in its functional organization and new operating procedures in all of its components. Commanders and their staffs were encouraged to eliminate functions and sections which had outlived their usefulness. The development of new functional organization and more efficient operating procedures was strongly encouraged throughout the entire period of the conflict and, indeed, was a necessity in order to cope effectively with the constantly changing tactical situation. Operating procedures and functional organization were based on the current situation and assigned mission. Procedures or organization which detracted from the optimum accomplishment of that mission were promptly discarded and new ones developed which would accomplish the mission effectively and efficiently.

Mobility, closely analogous and second in importance only to flexibility, is another prime prerequisite. To a tactical air force mobility on the ground is what flexibility is in the air. Fundamental to the mobility of a tactical air force is the provision of airfields where, when, and of types required by the tactical commands and administrative elements most effectively to carry out their respective tasks. In the IX Engineer Command the Ninth Air Force possessed a unique tool, which was designed specifically to develop to the maximum the mobility of tactical air operations. The Ninth Air Force was organized, trained and equipped so that its headquarters and tactical units could move individually or collectively at a moment's notice. All major units were organized into mobile and streamlined components, which could contribute to the flexibility, speed and striking power of the whole.

The role of tactical air power in the war in western Europe was that of air partner in an overwhelmingly powerful air-ground team, which (with the aid of the naval forces during the initial period of the assault on the beaches of Normandy and subsequent period of supply) had the mission of crushing the outer defenses of "Fortress Europe" and smashing to the heart of Germany. The Ninth Air Force and 12th Army Group formed a superbly cooperating team that achieved air-ground successes far exceeding the most optimistic estimates of our leading experts in this field. Their combined power was the dominating factor in the Allied war machine's swift defeat of the hitherto invincible German armies in western Europe.

As the air component of a tactical air-ground striking force it was logical for broad operational control of the Ninth Air Force to be exercised by Supreme Headquarters, Allied Expeditionary Forces, through its air staff section. However, administrative control was vested in the United States Strategic Air Forces in Europe. The division of responsibilities for the control of the tactical air force worked out "satisfactorily" at best. The urgency of operational, administrative and supply problems and requirements, during a rapidly changing tactical situation, needed, for a prompt, sound and proper solution, careful analysis and close coordination by *one* superior agency. With split responsibilities, operations were occasionally hindered and maximum exploitation of any given situation rendered unlikely. Too little (coordination) and too late (action), either operationally or administratively, are fatal to the successful exploitation of tactical air warfare. It was the considered conclusion of the Ninth Air Force that, from the standpoint of attaining maximum efficiency and effectiveness in the conduct of the tactical air war, the air force would have benefited immeasurably if there had been separate, co-equal air and ground headquarters at theater level, closely coordinating their operations but remaining independently responsible to the Supreme Commander.

The following chart illustrates the channels of command under which the Ninth Air Force was controlled operationally and administratively:

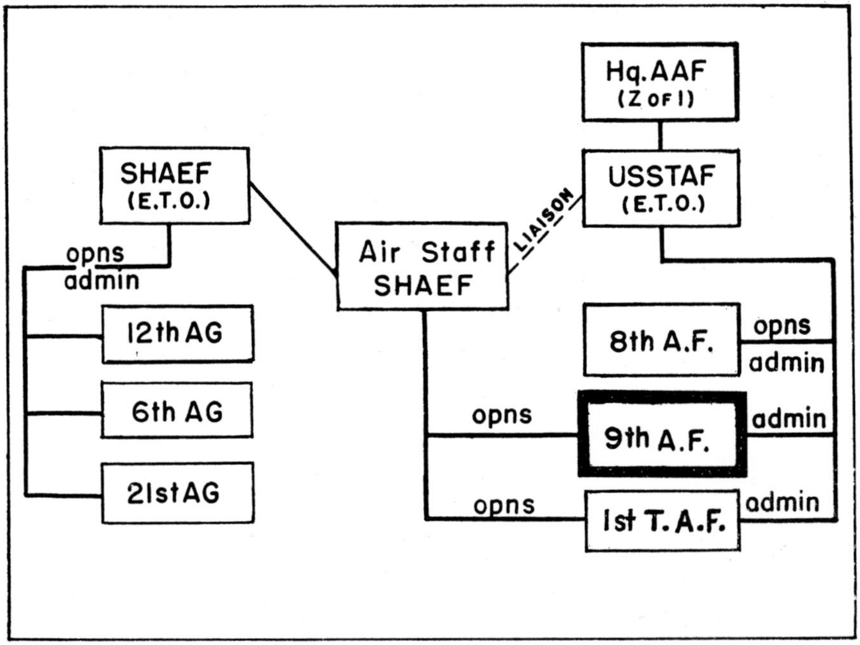

This highly condensed publication is essentially the text of chapter VIII, "Conclusions and Recommendations," Volume I of the study, "The Ninth Air Force and its Principal Commands in the European Theater of Operations—Operating Procedures and Functional Organization," augmented with sufficient narrative detail to make it self-contained. The nine volumes of the study are shortly scheduled for final processing and preparation for publication as a special study by Headquarters, Army Air Forces. Briefly, these volumes analyse the development of the operating procedures and functional organization of Headquarters Ninth Air Force, of its seven principal commands and of reconnaissance in the air force. However, these volumes are analytical *studies* and are not to be confused with any written history of the Ninth Air Force.

Chapter VIII, Volume I, of that study consists of a summarization of the major conclusions and recommendations selected throughout the entire study for their general air force interest and significance. These conclusions and recommendations form chapter IV and V of this publication. They cover the basic external relationships as well as the internal organizational structure and operating procedures of the tactical air force and its various components.

Much of the material presented herein is thought-provoking and the solutions to particular problems may, to some, appear to be questionable or even controversial. However, the material in this publication is derived from many months of careful study and analysis by those officers who commanded and staffed the Ninth Air Force and its subordinate commands during the actual period of conflict. The sum total of their findings was thoroughly considered, modified as necessary and finally approved by successive boards of experienced combat officers in the Headquarters Ninth Air Force and each command. The conclusions and recommendations, as here presented, represent those points upon which there was relative unanimity of opinion within the air force.

These conclusions and recommendations have been carefully studied and considered by Headquarters, United States Air Forces in Europe. They were concurred in with the following exceptions: (1) Reference to the division of air force headquarters (p. 112): "It is the opinion of Headquarters, USAFE, that any structure which splits administrative and operational jurisdiction for a period in excess of 30 days is basically unsound. Command, as such, can only be exercised over a prolonged period through utilization of both administrative and operational channels of jurisdiction and responsibility." (2) Reference to the organization of AAA (Page 110): "It is the opinion of Headquarters, USAFE, that certain automatic and dual-purpose ground and air weapons should be organic army equipment, the employment of which, in an anti-aircraft role in the forward areas, should be coordinated at the tactical air command-army level."

This publication is a special study intended to serve as a reference text for the various service schools which teach either fundamental or advanced courses on the organization and application of air power, as well as a guide to all concerned with current and future air force planning, policy and doctrine. It should prove particularly valuable to all agencies directly or indirectly concerned with the functional organization and operational procedures forged in combat by a tactical air force. This publication has been prepared, published and distributed with the approval and authorization of the Headquarters, AAF. However, such approval and authorization do not necessarily establish this material as approved Army Air Forces doctrine.

The facts and considerations presented in this study were drawn from Ninth Air Force experience under the specific tactical conditions and situations which existed in the European Theater of Operations. It is thoroughly appreciated that tactical air forces in other theaters may have reached widely differing conclusions on certain of the subjects considered in this study. These conclusions and recommendations are those of the Ninth Air Force and are not intended to reflect the opinions of other tactical air forces.

It is considered that the most equitable method of ascertaining the total results of all the experience gained by the various tactical air forces would be through convening a board of experienced tactical and administrative experts who would represent the various tactical air forces. The purpose of this board would be to consider the various aspects of the tactical air war with a view to revising and bringing up to date all manuals dealing with the organization and application of tactical air power. It is further suggested that consideration be given to inviting British tactical air experts to sit on any such board in an advisory capacity.

Chapter II

A CRITICAL REVIEW OF OPERATIONS

A. GENERAL OPERATIONAL CONSIDERATIONS

THE MISSION of the Ninth Air Force in the European Theater of Operations was the general mission of tactical air forces, defined in FM 100–20, "Command and Employment of Air Power": Priority 1: to gain and maintain air superiority; Priority 2: to disrupt hostile lines of communication; Priority 3: to destroy enemy troops and matériel on the fighting front in cooperation with forward ground forces. (Note that throughout this report these are referred to respectively as Phase 1, Phase 2 and Phase 3 operations.)

This concept of the employment of tactical air power, which proved absolutely sound in the combat experience of the Ninth Air Force, is as interesting for what it omits as for what it contains. Long-range, deep attacks on enemy production centers and large cities in the rear were not part of the tactical air job. On the contrary, the tactical air force was engaged directly against elements of the enemy's manufactured and trained war machine (its personnel, matériel, transport, shelter and fortifications) either in or on the way to the fighting zone. The speed with which the Ninth Air Force frequently had to plan and execute operations, the variable strength of the operational unit (depending upon the size and vulnerability of the target) and the relatively short range, with multiple "turn-around" missions, at which fighter-bombers were normally applied, imposed a set of organizational necessities which were not encountered on a comparable scale by any other American air force.

The fact that the Ninth Air Force's field of operation was limited to the front and the immediate enemy rear must not be misinterpreted to indicate that the operations themselves were of limited intensity or value. Actually a huge force could be and was employed profitably in the tactical zone of operation. The volume, extent and scale of tactical operations necessary to accomplish the three phases of the mission can be visualized only with the realization that at one time the

Ninth was numerically the strongest air force in the world, that in good flying weather it averaged as many as 2,000 sorties a day and that its bases in 19 months of combat advanced across the English Channel and thence several hundred miles through 6 countries.

Another determining factor in the development of the Ninth Air Force was that from the start it was intended for operational partnership with an American army group (the 1st, later the 12th) and its component armies. To achieve complete air-ground cooperation it was imperative that the Ninth Air Force be organized: (1) to move expeditiously to the continent in the earliest possible stages of Operation OVERLORD, (2) to service and supply all its units initially across 90 miles of open water and subsequently over the continent as they spread over a rapidly extending and advancing front hundreds of miles long, (3) to conduct active air defense behind the entire American front, (4) to construct or rehabilitate all airfields required in the rear and forward areas, (5) to design all tactical and service units so that their mobility would approximate that of the ground units with which they were associated, (6) to develop and maintain an operational flexibility permitting immediate application of all or any part of the tactical striking force at any point or series of points on the long front to a depth of up to 200 miles and (7) to develop and perfect a highly sensitive system of tactical control of airborne aircraft to achieve precise coordination of air effort with any phase of the ground effort.

This complex operational commitment—combining power with sensitivity, mobility with continuity of operation, and flexibility with full, economical employment of the available force—determined the unconventional structure of the Ninth Air Force and its seven major commands. The very names and types of the commands illustrate clearly the many-sided nature of the Ninth Air Force's operational program, which was as fluid and as intricate as the war itself.

The air force's principal weapon was the fighter-bomber—armed with bombs, bullets and frequently with rockets and chemical fire bombs—which was capable of highly rapid diversion through radar and VHF control means to the most profitable targets and which maintained excellent air-to-ground communications with armored and infantry spearheads actually engaged in battle and potentially, if not almost continually, desiring or requiring cooperation from the air. The fighter-bomber, the most familiar aircraft to infantrymen and tankers on the line, was effective in the accomplishment of all three phases of the mission. Without its bombs it was a powerful, dangerous fighter, which outmatched the German Air Force in the air whenever they met. With bombs and machine guns it destroyed thousands of enemy aircraft and air installations on or near airfields to complete its contribution to the attainment of air superiority. In Phase 2 operations the fighter-bomber was most remuneratively employed in isolation of the tactical sphere of operations by attacks on enemy road and rail lines and transport on the move anywhere along these lines. Backed by a highly developed system of tactical radar control and excellent air-ground communications which permitted immediate reaction to developments in the air and on the ground, the fighter-bomber was the most effective aircraft of the war in close-in cooperation with ground elements and in the neutralization or destruction of enemy personnel, matériel and installations in the immediate battle area.

The fighter-bomber was the basic striking component of the three tactical air commands of the Ninth Air Force. Within the broad air force-army group partnership these commands maintained operational partnership with their associated armies. A relatively new type of AAF organization, the tactical air command was assigned a variable number of fighter-bomber groups (normally four to eight) and one reconnaissance group and it was responsible for fighter-bomber operations and for routine daily reconnaissance in cooperation with its associated army. Although the TACs were granted unusual latitude in control of their tactical units, air force control was never allowed to become superficial. Air force retained full prerogative to shift forces from one TAC to another or to combine and employ the forces of all TACs on any one of several fronts when necessary to implement air force-army group plans or to meet critical situations at any point in the army group area. On its army front the TAC in turn apportioned its available force to cooperative operations with corps and divisions or to Phase 1 and 2 operations as the situation demanded. Thus with intimate association from the highest to the lowest levels of army and air force command, 12th Army Group and Ninth Air Force worked out a most sensitive and effective air-ground team.

The air force's medium and light bombers, which, like the fighter-bombers, formed the largest single force of their type in the USAAF, were organized and employed quite differently. The bombers were not used in routine daily operations based on the tactical requirements of any particular army, nor were they assigned to or divided among the tactical air commands. Experience proved that they were employed most effectively in Phase 2 precision-bombing operations against static targets, such as communications centers, bridges, and railway yards and against such objectives as supply depots and fuel and ammunition dumps. The relative importance of these targets could best be measured at air force level and their systematic destruction planned and executed only after a thorough appraisal of the tactical situation over the entire army group front, with a view to meeting most efficiently and effectively the total air force commitment. Medium and light bombardment was preserved as a single striking force which, however, was often divided to attack many targets simultaneously. The air force's medium of control of these aircraft was 9th Bombardment Division.

The Ninth Air Force's fifth "operational" command, in the pure sense of a command which actually struck at the enemy, was the IX Air Defense Command, the first of its kind assigned to any U. S. air force during World War II. Although the establishment of an air defense command was delayed and actually was conceived as an afterthought, the responsibility clearly belonged to the Ninth Air Force to help fulfill the first priority commitment, maintenance of air superiority by defense of the air element against intrusion by the enemy. The command,.which participated in counter-air force operations and was particularly successful in counter-V bomb operations, was equipped with signal air warning systems and with various types of air defense weapons, including a heavy proportion of antiaircraft artillery. Its initial operations were hampered by a confused interpretation by both air and ground of the distinction between air force and ground force responsibilities for antiaircraft defense. Experience gained during the campaign dictated the solution which was finally applied, whereby ground force AA protected ground force elements in the forward battle area while air force AA protected all else.

The IX Engineer Command was another new command, created for effective operational control and administration of more than 20,000 aviation engineer personnel. This command was responsible for developing, constructing and rehabilitating air fields and installations which would enable Ninth Air Force units to be applied most rapidly and destructively against the enemy. The effectiveness of a tactical air force increases directly with the proximity of its bases to the front lines. It was recognized early in the planning that the greatest single limiting factor on the ability of the Ninth Air Force to carry out its mission would be the speed with which air bases could be brought into operation behind the advancing ground forces. The magnitude and technical nature of this task, together with the attendant supply, maintenance and purely administrative problems, led to the decision by Lt. (then Maj.) Gen. Lewis H. Brereton to place full responsibility for these tasks on a self-sufficient engineer command, with full command and administrative authority over its assigned units. The command, throughout the war on the continent, maintained an unusually hazardous and difficult advance, with forward elements of the ground forces, to survey, secure, and prepare bases in the most forward areas under enemy observation and fire.

The Ninth Air Force's seventh and largest major command was the nominally conventional IX Air Force Service Command with 60,000 officers and men. However, because of the mobility and flexibility of the entire air force, the service command was faced with many unusual problems, as well as the constant responsibility of maintaining supply and maintenance service along rapidly lengthening lines of communications over a 90-mile stretch of sea and hundreds of miles of land. Maintenance and supply, under the conditions of operation of the Ninth Air Force, were definitely not the fixed, predictable problems which they are for a more settled air force. Consequently the service command was compelled to work out its functional organization and operating procedures with little regard for patterns or precedents.

Up to the early autumn of 1944 the IX Troop Carrier Command occupied an extremely important position in the air force. Under the Ninth Air Force the troop carrier command organized, planned and successfully executed the greatest troop-carrier operation in history, the delivery of paratroops and airborne units behind the German lines on the Cherbourg Peninsula, and maintained resupply and medical evacuation operations for several months after D-day. All the early plans had conceived the troop-carrier function as part of the tactical air mission, falling into Phase 3, but when the airborne and paratroop forces reached the proportions of an army the Supreme Commander decided to unite them and troop-carrier aircraft under a single "airborne army" command responsible directly to SHAEF. Consequently the IX Troop

Carrier Command was transferred to the First Allied Airborne Army approximately three months after D-day.

B. PRE-INVASION TACTICAL AIR OFFENSIVE (16 October 1943–5 June 1944)

The pre-invasion activities of the Ninth Air Force were marked by a very rapid physical growth, exceedingly intricate and detailed organizational planning and experiment and, during the latter months of the period, large-scale "softening up" operations against continental installations to pave the way for invasion.

During the first few months after its reconstitution in the United Kingdom under the command of Lt. Gen. Lewis H. Brereton the Ninth Air Force concentrated on activating, organizing, training and equipping the many specialized tactical, technical and service units which would function as a huge, smoothly working team in Operation OVERLORD and thereafter. Planned to be the major air component of the Allied invasion forces, the Ninth from 16 October 1943 until D-day had a remarkably rapid physical growth: from 4 to 45 tactical groups, from less than 300 to more than 1,100 bombers, from zero to more than 3,000 troop-carrier aircraft and gliders and from fewer than 50,000 to considerably more than 200,000 personnel. While this development was unusually rapid it must not be supposed that it was a simple automatic process without great obstacles or delays. The job of the Ninth Air Force was not primarily to fit organized, trained, and equipped units into its structure but rather to construct these units from casual personnel, to struggle for their aircraft or other equipment and to train and retrain all personnel for functions quite often entirely foreign to those for which they were originally trained and equipped.

It is appropriate that this review indicate only certain of the major difficulties which the Ninth Air Force surmounted in building to full strength. For instance, the original organizational plan for the tactical air force in the ETO (the Bradley Plan) anticipated only two air headquarters to cooperate with ground armies. It failed to provide personnel for the additional operational air headquarters which were required to cooperate with the 12th Army Group and its four armies. Furthermore, it made no provision for such essential units as tactical air liaison parties, all-weather bombing units, tactical weather reconnaissance and night photographic reconnaissance squadrons. Allocations of personnel for military police and security duties and basic functions were inadequate. The Ninth Air Force, in each case, found it necessary later to improvise and to manipulate tables of organization and equipment in order to make up for such inadequacies.

A problem which became increasingly difficult as the war continued was the inadequate pre-combat training of crews arriving in the theater and the necessity of establishing training programs and schools within the various commands and particularly within the IX Air Force Service Command, thereby detracting materially from the over-all operational effort. Other personnel difficulties arose because of an impractical policy which resulted in the shipment of large numbers of casual personnel to the theater without adequate consideration of the MOS required by the air force, a serious shortage of professionally qualified intelligence officers for higher staffs and lack of a policy preventing the separation of specialist personnel from their highly specialized equipment when they were sent to the theater, e. g., MEWs and their operators and mechanics. These—and other basic personnel problems involving the activation and organization of unconventional but essential units—are considered more fully in the following chapter on Administration, but they may be mentioned here as delaying factors in the physical and operational growth of the Ninth Air Force.

In addition to its own build-up the Ninth Air Force during this period had the responsibility of establishing parallel plans and training programs and setting up intimate operational and administrative liaison with 1st U. S. Army Group, in order to insure that air and ground would operate with a maximum understanding of each other's capabilities and limitations. Air operations had to be "all-out" prior to, on and subsequent to D-day. Efficient and effective coordination of the air-ground effort required that the air-ground liaison be letter perfect. In planning a tactical air campaign of the magnitude necessary in the European theater the Ninth Air Force again had no precise models for guidance and very limited USAAF experience upon which to draw.

Long before D-day it was apparent to Ninth Air Force commanders and staff officers that FM 31–35, "Aviation in Support of Ground Forces," had become obsolete and wholly inadequate. The manual did not visualize the flexibility and mobility needed and developed by the tactical air force. It had no real conception of the ultimate capabilities of "cooperative" air operations in conjunction with the ground effort or of the tremendous value and potentialities of visual, tactical, photographic and artillery-adjustment reconnaissance. In practice, Ninth Air Force had to pioneer its own tactical air cooperation and form its command and inter-command relationships and structure, based on the limited experience of the RAF and three groups of P–40s and two groups of B–25s of the Ninth Air Force in the Middle East—Cyrenaica and Libya.

The lack of co-equal air and ground headquarters at theater level and the fact that theater operational control was exercised by one headquarters (Air Staff, SHAEF) and administrative control by another (USSTAF) were from the start detrimental to the efficient functioning of the air force. Some of the results of this confusing situation were an inadequate representation of air officers experienced in tactical operations at the top headquarters and occasionally inequitable distribution of available personnel, non-uniform interpretation of operational and administrative policies for air forces in the theater and inadequate liaison between certain of the air and ground forces. The appointment of Maj. Gen. David M. Schlatter as senior American air force officer with Air Staff SHAEF was extremely helpful to the Ninth Air Force, for he constantly clarified and presented the plans, requirements and problems of the tactical air force to the Supreme Commander.

In direct contacts and associations with the army group and the armies (which were, unfortunately, limited before invasion), the Ninth Air Force initially found itself at considerable disadvantage because of the disparity in rank between air and ground commanders and their staffs and because of the lack of a War Department statement of policy as to which air and ground headquarters would be considered as co-equal. Although there were no pre-defined channels of liaison for air force and army group in the build-up period, in practice the Ninth Air Force and 1st (later redesignated 12th) Army Group were able to work out an excellent *modus operandi* based on the equality of the two headquarters as military elements and the necessity for future liaison down to comparatively low levels of command. The very excellent close cooperation which later characterized the operations of the TAC-army teams on the continent was to some extent foreshadowed in combined air-ground exercises and in a restricted amount of combined planning for Phase 3 operations before the invasion.

In an effort to anticipate some of the problems which would arise on the continent the Ninth Air Force early adopted a policy of planning and organizing for a maximum of the mobility and flexibility which would be necessary in combined operations. The first step—a fundamental departure from conventional AAF headquarters organization—was to form a compact, highly mobile advanced headquarters which would move forward on the same axis of communications as, and always remain in close proximity to, army group headquarters, no matter how swiftly it moved. This advanced headquarters would handle all air force operations independently of the larger administrative headquarters. The first advanced detachment was organized in October 1943 and engaged in mobile field exercises in the United Kingdom for a month. From that time on, considerable progress was made in testing and re-testing, under simulated and actual combat conditions, the organization and composition of the forward echelon until, on 5 August 1944, it was prepared for full, active cooperation with Headquarters 12th Army Group in the drive from France to the Elbe, Czechoslovakia, and Austria.

Although in the autumn of 1943 and the winter of 1943–44 the Ninth Air Force emphasized build-up and planning, it simultaneously carried out medium bomber and long-range fighter operations, which formed a comparatively small but significant part of the air campaign from Britain. The first phase of these operations, which had been initiated by medium bombers before the reconstitution of the Ninth Air Force in Britain, was a series of diversionary attacks on the belt of German coastal airfields in France, Belgium and Holland which were used as bases for enemy fighters opposing the passage of Eighth Air Force heavy bombers. Although the medium bomber force was small and although the necessity for contact flying both in target and base areas restricted the number of operational days, these counter-air force operations contributed materially to forcing the Luftwaffe to draw its fighters inland, where they represented a less serious threat not only to the "heavies" but to the invasion forces which were to arrive in Normandy on 6 June 1944.

The airfield targets—and the "cross-bow" and "no-ball" rocket bomb targets which were publicly identified only as military objectives—were the main preoccupation of the Ninth's bomber force until February 1944, when the stress shifted to railway centers surrounding and connecting the possible invasion points.

Meanwhile, starting on 1 December 1943, the Ninth Air Force introduced the first long-range fighter aircraft into the air offensive and by mid-winter the improved P–51B Mustangs of the 354th Fighter Group were regularly accompanying Eighth Air Force heavy bombers over their targets deep in Germany. The new Mustangs proved magnificently successful in aerial combat, constantly meeting and defeating superior forces of German aircraft which theatened the heavy bomber formations.

Shortly after the redesignation of the IX Air Support Command as the IX Tactical Air Command fighter control centers were placed in operation at Middle Wallop and Biggin Hill. The fighter control centers were RAF focal points for the control of all aircraft operating in the area of southern England. Both heavy- and light-weight radars were placed in operation at strategic points along the southern coast and an efficient DF net was established. Inasmuch as these centers were operated primarily for and by the RAF, American fighter control personnel were placed on duty at both of these centers for the handling of AAF strike missions. This was done because it was considered inadvisable to place our aircraft under British jurisdiction and control.

Although Ninth Air Force operations continued to be of a harassing and subordinate character until early May 1944, a shift in emphasis as early as February foreshadowed the violent tactical air campaign that was to be waged the last 5 weeks before D-day. Bombardment directives began to include many of the marshalling yards and railway centers connecting the German anti-invasion coastal defenses with arsenals and troop centers in the enemy interior. This first interdiction campaign was necessarily carefully planned not to reveal the location of the invasion thrust and, more positively, to confuse the enemy about the intentions of the Allied Expeditionary Forces. The bombers at the same time maintained operations against V-bomb launching sites in the Pas de Calais and adjacent areas with an effectiveness which Air Chief Marshal Sir Trafford Leigh-Mallory cited in this statement: "Of all the bomber forces involved, those of the Ninth Air Force proved to be by far the most efficacious in knocking out these difficult and defended targets."

As the bomber force grew and expanded its sphere of operations the Ninth Air Force introduced revolutionary innovations in the employment of fighters. With the addition of bombs and later of rockets the offensive power of Ninth Air Force fighters developed enormously and gradually escort and other primarily defensive operations were abandoned in favor of hard-hitting, offensive operations over the future area of ground operations.

By May 1944 the air force had grown very nearly to full strength and was prepared to assume a full share of the responsibility for pre-invasion accomplishment of Phase 1 and 2 objectives. In May the Ninth Air Force dispatched an average of more than 1,000 aircraft daily against enemy lines of communication leading into and supporting the Atlantic wall defenses, both in the Calais and the Normandy areas, and against all types of enemy transport on rails, roads and rivers, to prevent supply, reinforcement and re-fortification of the vital sectors.

As the invasion approached IX Bomber Command and the two existing tactical air commands, the IX and XIX, were given full responsibility for a systematic program of interdiction which called for the destruction of all major railway and highway bridges crossing the Seine from Paris to the English Channel—isolating Normandy and Brittany in the west from Pas de Calais and the Low Countries' coast in the east. This program was pursued until only one road bridge was serviceable between Conflans and Rouen and the enemy was forced to follow circuitous, slow, and costly routes to move troops and supplies to the beaches. At the same time the bombardment force began late in the spring to carry out difficult precision bombing attacks against the large anti-invasion guns in use or under construction on the French coast.

Reconnaissance, daily becoming increasingly important in the tactical sphere of operations, was fitted into the total air force operational scheme in order to provide vast quantities of detailed intelligence to the ground forces for the assault stage, as well as to furnish clues for most effective bomber and fighter-bomber employment. High reconnaissance, for instance, revealed extensive beach defense construction on the French shore, while low (10 to 50 feet true altitude), extremely hazardous "dicing" missions undertaken by the 10th Photo Reconnaissance Group accomplished possibly the war's most remarkable and valuable photography, by providing close-range, easily interpreted photographs of the intimate details of the beach defenses along the full length of the potential invasion coast, including the Calais sector.

In May IX Troop Carrier Command carried out the enormous Exercise EAGLE in preparation for the delivery of paratroops and airborne infantry to the Cherbourg Peninsula to touch off the invasion. Also in May IX Air Defense Command assumed responsibility for the antiaircraft defense, both of the air force's tactical bases and of the large, vulnerable troop-carrier installations scattered over southern England.

The IX Engineer Command meanwhile was perfecting its headquarters organization, assemblying equipment and training its units on loan from SOS, where they were engaged in construction of heavy bomber fields. Simultaneously it was constructing its own concentration areas and preparing advance landing grounds on the south coast of England as bases of operation for units of the tactical air commands during the early stages of the invasion.

During the entire pre-invasion period the Ninth Air Force stressed continually the importance of mobility in all of its tactical units. Although in the United Kingdom bombers and fighter-bombers operated from relatively fixed bases, all personnel were trained for speeedy removal to the continent and for rapid movement subsequently in order to follow the ground force advance closely. Constant checks were made at all levels to assure that units were not becoming excessively deeply rooted at their bases or accumulating equipment which could not be put on wheels. In the last few days before invasion fighter-bomber groups moved to these advance landing grounds, where they operated under conditions closely approximating those they would meet on the continent.

Immediately prior to D-day it was concluded that the existing system of transmitting operational orders by teletype from Uxbridge (IX Fighter Command and Ninth Air Force Advanced Headquarters) to the tactical groups was too slow. To overcome this operations officers were placed on duty at both the Middle Wallop and Biggin Hill fighter control centers to facilitate the passage of strike requests from the air force to the groups and to make "on-the-spot" combat decisions relative to the control of aircraft in flight. This actually was the embryo of the future combat operations—tactical control group "marriage" which later occurred in France. During this period all fighter wings under the Ninth Air Force had aircraft control and warning personnel assigned in order to maintain a fighter control center at each wing. These, however, were not utilized until the landings were made, whereupon the 70th Fighter Wing set up fighter control facilities ("Sweepstakes") which took over all Ninth Air Force aircraft control and warning functions of both the Middle Wallop and Biggin Hill centers.

C. CAMPAIGN OF NORMANDY (6 June 1944–24 July 1944)

D-day brought with it no break in the continuity of Ninth Air Force operations. Counter-air force and interdiction programs continued throughout the pre-invasion, invasion and post-invasion periods. The success of these programs was most apparent in the first days of the assault, when the German Air Force failed to oppose either the cross-channel movement of the landings with any appreciable power and when the German army was unable to swing into line with the promptness and ease required. In other fields, however, D-day put the Ninth Air Force to its first tests in mobility, in intimate cooperation with the armies in the field, in control of aircraft by shipborne radar and in rapid adjustment to highly variable tactical ground situations.

German air and ground commanders almost unanimously agreed that the air force was the decisive factor in the ability of the Allied Expeditionary Forces to secure a lodgement on the beaches of Normandy and to expand and strengthen their assault forces until it became impossible for the Germans to drive the Allies into the sea. To quote Herman Goering: "The Allies owe the success of the invasion to their air forces. They prepared the invasion; they made it possible; and they carried it through."

The tactical air contribution to the invasion was manifold, but perhaps its two main features were: (1) operations which prevented the Germans from shifting their forces rapidly or effectively enough to meet the threat and from building up forces in Normandy at a rate equivalent to the Allied build-up and (2) the overwhelming air superiority which denied use of the air to the enemy and insured completely unrestricted movement behind and into the lines by the Allied ground forces.

The commitments of the Ninth Air Force on D-day were vast and intricate. The troop carrier command delivered paratroops and airborne infantry behind the German lines on the Cherbourg Peninsula as the opening blow in the greatest military operation in history. Medium and light bombers, taking off before dawn, carried out eleventh-hour attacks against powerful German defensive gun batteries on Utah beach and later in the day switched to communications centers, command posts, supply depots and other targets in the enemy's immediate rear. First U. S. Army reported that enemy coastal defenses were much less formidable than had been expected, that in fact this section of the European Fortress was no fortress at all, and it attributed much of this surprising weakness to the power of tactical air attacks on the shore before and during D-day.

Flying approximately 2,300 sorties in 20 hours fighter-bombers had the general commitments of protecting the cross-channel movement, preparing the way for landings by neutralizing beach defenses, protecting troops actually on the beaches, reducing the enemy's ability to mount an effective counter-attack by denying him the use of roads into the battle area and, finally, providing full Phase 3 cooperation in the advance of ground forces inland from the assault areas. The effectiveness of the purely protective phase of this assignment was evident in the failure of the German Air Force to oppose the invasion. The effectiveness of the interdiction campaign has been proved by scores of reports from captured German commanders, describing the difficulty of travelling on all roads leading to the front in daylight, the necessity of using aircraft spotters on all vehicles and the failure of troops to reach their positions in the line at full strength, on time or in an orderly fashion. Representative of these is the story told by General Fritz Bayerlain, commander of the crack Panzer Lehr division, who said that his unit took 80 hours to make a 12-hour trip to the front and arrived with only 50 percent of its original firepower. Von Rundstedt complained, too, that the incessant fighter-bomber attacks on roads and rails, as well as the bomber attacks on larger communications centers, prevented the shifting of reserves which could have defeated the Allies on the beaches.

In addition to attacks with paratroops, airborne troops and bombs and bullets the Ninth Air Force generally had an enormous reconnaissance job on D-day. A seriously overworked and newly formed night photo reconnaissance squadron, the only unit of its kind with the air force during the war, photographed the beaches and the area just behind them on the night of 5–6 June. The value of this squadron's work at that time and later was great and it underlined the need for a particularly well trained and completely equipped night photo reconnaissance squadron in each of the tactical air commands, as well as one serving air force headquarters. From early morning until late evening tactical and photo reconnaissance aircraft flew in a continual stream across the channel, to record every movement of the enemy and assess the damage wrought upon him. Reconnaissance in general, however, was very poorly provided for in preliminary plans for the air force and it became obvious as the war progressed that the need for visual, tactical, photographic, artillery and night reconnaissance required that a minimum of one reconnaissance group be assigned to each of the TACs. There eventually proved also to be an urgent requirement for the assignment of a reconnaissance group to air force headquarters to carry out requirements for reconnaissance of all types required at air force-army group level and higher.

The first units of IX Engineer Command landed on Utah beach on D-day and on Omaha beach on D plus 1. An emergency landing strip was completed on Utah by 2115 hours on D-day. On Omaha the pre-planned construction sites were still in enemy hands when engineer troops became available on D plus 1, so a new site was selected at St. Laurent-sur-Mer and an unscheduled transport field was made operational by noon of D plus 3. The build-up of aviation engineer units proceeded approximately on schedule: by D plus 5 four battalions were ashore and construction was well under way on three fighter-bomber airfields on Omaha and one on Utah. The speed and effectiveness of the engineer command under Brig. Gen. James B. Newman, Jr., were evident in its accomplishments during the build-up period. By D plus 16 five fighter-bomber groups were based in Normandy and participated in the all-out air assault on the outer defenses of Cherbourg. By 30 June (D plus 24) nine all-weather airfields had been completed on the continent and seven others were under construction.

In the first days of the battle of Europe the Ninth Air Force improvised and then improved a system of close radar control of tactical air units employing a variety of control procedures and radar devices until a system of positive control which was sound and efficient in combat was devised. During the assault IX TAC controllers on offshore ships maintained close radar and voice control of all tactical air operations. Once established on the beach the IX TAC, commanded by Maj. Gen. E. R. Quesada, took over operational and administrative control of all tactical units from the moment they reached the beach until air force advanced headquarters became operational on the continent. The first air control station on the beach was established by 70th Fighter Wing, which sent an advanced detachment to function with First Army until the arrival of the TAC's forward headquarters. Almost immediately, however, the TAC itself set up an advanced headquarters component adjacent to the First Army CP and, although air force also sent over an advanced element on 8 June, it was not until the first part of August that IX TAC relinquished operational control of any continent-based Ninth Air Force units.

A certain amount of time was required for air force and army group to "shake down" the carefully planned but operationally untested mission request system and work out a thoroughly satisfactory system for mission requests and priorities. The first machinery was not completely smooth or adequate. Medium bombardment mision requests initially were routed from subordinate ground units to army headquarters and then to 21st Army Group Headquarters in England, where they were transmitted to the air force. Urgent requests proceeded directly from the tactical air liaison officers with ground units to 21st Army Group. During this period IX TAC accepted or rejected all requests for fighter-bomber effort without recourse to air force. At this time the principle of close-column cover, and the ground-to-plane VHF communications which made it possible, was not yet fully accepted by the ground forces and even some air force circles were dubious of its value. This lack was felt keenly by forward ground units and by TALOs (tactical air liaison officers, formerly air support party officers). Each TAC developed its own descriptive titles for these parties, using BACU, AGCO and TALO; however, TALO became most commonly used and will be used throughout this study for clarity. It later became standard procedure for TALOs, as operations representatives of the tactical air commander, to direct aircraft from one target to another after they had become airborne, if those aircraft had been ordered to report into that forward ground station or if an emergency situation existed on the ground in that area. Initially, however, the air officers with frontline ground units were forced to persuade and cajole squadron commanders to divert their force from assigned to unassigned objectives. The decision as to whether any target of opportunity would be attacked upon radio requests from ground units rested with the commander of the aircraft over the target.

From 6 June to 24 July the Ninth Air Force concentrated upon maintaining undiminished operations against the enemy in cooperation with ground forces and upon transferring tactical units to the continent as rapidly as possible. By the end of the period 13 fighter-bomber groups and one reconnaissance group had crossed the channel and a highly efficient and effective radar control system had been established on the beach-head without losing a single day of operations. Continuing to operate from Britain, medium and light bombers relentlessly smashed bridges over the Seine and Loire Rivers, attacked railway yards and communications centers and destroyed fuel and ammunition supply points serving the Germans along the entire Allied front in Normandy.

It had been envisioned in initial planning that each tactical air command would have more than one control center operating simultaneously. It was soon discovered in actual combat, however, that by implementing the 70th Fighter Wing control center with sufficient radar equipment and personnel to permit "leap-frog" operations one fighter control center could adequately handle all aircraft control and warning functions for one tactical air command. This was a further step towards the consolidation of all existing aircraft control and warning devices of each TAC into a single tactical aircraft control and warning group.

On 22 June, the most spectacular day of operations since D-day, a massive air bombing assault, including all available fighter bombers, was launched against German fortifications and entrenched troops defending Cherbourg. The air attack went off moderately well and shook up the defending forces considerably. The medium bombers did excellent work and were properly employed. The principle of employing fighter-bombers to cooperate with a large-scale ground effort was sound; however, their employment in strafing and bombing area targets in a close-cooperation operation without a medium of on-the-spot ground control and without specific knowledge of their objectives was considered one of the few significant misapplications of tactical air power in the entire career of the Ninth Air Force in the European Theater of Operations.

When the plan for the 22 June air operation at Cherbourg was drawn up, it was acknowledged that the use of fighter-bombers in such a role would not contribute materially to the effectiveness of the air assault, particularly in view of the lack of adequate communications between the forces in Normandy and the bulk of the participating air units which were then still based in Britain. Another detrimental factor was the lack both of mobile ground-to-air communications and of specific knowledge of the target area. Further, the fact that the air force received fewer than 24 hours advance notice of the combined assault made it almost certain that a large portion of the fighter-bomber effort would be wasted.

Although these obvious disadvantages were recognized before the operation, they were considered outweighed by the necessity for keeping the American ground offensive moving toward the port of Cherbourg. The Cherbourg air assault as finally executed, although expensive and essentially unsound, constituted a natural and circumstantially unavoidable step in the evolution of effective tactics and technique of fighter-bomber application. Approximately 25 fighter-bombers were lost in the operation. These losses were considered an excessive price to pay for the positive results which the Cherbourg air assault received. However, the operation had a great negative value in that it strongly impressed all the commanders and staffs concerned in the necessity for detailed planning, thorough coordination and complete understanding on the part of all participants before attempting major combined air-ground efforts. It also pointed out the necessity for executing at TAC-army level all detailed planning for air assaults and for close cooperation with ground attacks.

In the period between the capture of Cherbourg and Operation COBRA at St. Lo—a period which was described by the 12th Army Group as largely a struggle for "limited objectives"—the chief contribution of fighter-bombers was the almost total restriction of enemy movement and reinforcement during flyable daylight hours to a depth of approximately 30 kilometers behind the lines. Von Rundstedt reported to Berlin that "whenever assembly areas are detected, an attack by fighter-bombers is launched without delay." With the IX TAC combat operations and fighter control center exercising increasingly effective and precise control over airborne fighter-bombers by microwave early warning, fighter director posts and SCR–584, the planes were successful in attacks on strongpoints, troop formations, self-propelled guns, tanks, armored vehicles and field fortifications at the fighting front and drastically reduced the volume of enemy artillery fire by their mere threatening presence over the battle area. The "Jabos," as the German troops called fighter-bombers, were indeed the Allies' "most terrible weapon."

By 24 July 18 fighter-bomber and reconnaissance groups of the Ninth Air Force were fully operational from 15 bases in Normandy and additional airfields were under construction for 1 reconnaissance group and 4 light or medium bomber groups.

Shortly after D-day the IX Air Defense Command established itself on the continent and prepared to take over air defense responsibility from the IX TAC. Its operating agencies were two provisional air defense wings (U. S.) and two RAF sectors—each equipped with night fighters, fighter control and air warning services and capable of conducting air defense operations in a designated area. The first of such areas was the Cotentin Peninsula, to which 21 Sector, RAF, was assigned. The command also undertook its movement liaison function—the task of maintaining and dispensing up-to-the-minute information on all air traffic.

The problem of the coordination and control of AA artillery became acute during this period, complicated by the tremendous concentration of AAA in the beach-head and the mass of Allied aircraft overhead. At this time all AAA was under ground force command, a factor which contributed greatly to the lack of coordination and teamwork, which in turn resulted in insufficient air defense dispositions, the engagement of friendly aircraft by our own AAA and severe restrictions on flying and at times seriously interfered with the conduct of air operations. This unsatisfactory condition was remedied to a considerable extent after two months of operations, when the IX ADC was given command of all AAA behind the army rear boundary.

After a thorough study of all possible influencing factors over 12 months of operation the Ninth Air Force concluded the AAA defense must normally be considered an air force responsibility. The ground forces would then employ only a suitable complement of automatic air defense weapons to protect their own troops in the fighting zone. Regardless of the decision which may be reached on this matter, the tactical air commands must have complete responsibility and the necessary weapons for the air defense of their own forward installations and airfields in the army area. The tactical air unit must be "married" before combat to the AAA unit protecting its base and the two must be maintained together permanently in the course of one or a series of campaigns.

D. CAMPAIGN OF WESTERN FRANCE AND BRITTANY (25 July 1944–25 August 1944)

In its study, "Effects of Air Power on Military Operations, Western Europe," 12th Army Group concluded that Operation COBRA on 25 July "marked the begining of the most effectively sustained close air support in history." On that day an area 3,000 feet by 7,000 feet south of the St. Lo-Periers highway was saturated with clock-like precision and accuracy by the bombs of 1,500 heavies, 400 mediums and 550 fighter-bombers in 2½ hours. The shock effect of this massive effort on German troops was terrific. It completely disrupted enemy communications. Taking a lesson from the Cherbourg air bombardment, immediately after the air operation the ground forces proceeded to exploit the disorganization of the enemy and made the first major break-through since the invasion. All the American ground commanders agreed that their major difficulty in advancing after this tremendous aerial barrage was not from the negligible enemy resistance but rather from the incredibly cratered terrain.

Part of the preparation for Operation COBRA was highly significant: it marked the beginning of real close-in cooperation between the air and ground forces and pointed up the urgent need for better air planning and closer coordination of details of combined air-ground effort when strategic forces were to be brought into tactical play. Two-way very-high-frequency ground-air radio sets were installed in the lead tanks of all First Army spearheads, making possible instantaneous communication between forward ground elements and the fighter-bombers over them in the course of battle. Furthermore, to assure that requests from the ground were not unreasonable from the air force standpoint, highly qualified pilots rode with the very foremost elements of the tank columns to take charge of ground direction of aircraft and to advise ground commanders of the practicability of requested missions.

Meanwhile, on command level, the combined First Army–IX TAC operations center coordinated broad air-ground operations with increasing effectiveness. The result of these innovations in air-ground communication and forward control of aircraft was immediate and remunerative. During the remaining daylight hours of 25 July and on the following 2 days fighter-bombers flew armed reconnaissance west, south, and east of the break-through point to prevent a shifting of German reserves and to disorganize the retreat of withdrawing elements. Before the end of July more than 400 armored column cover missions had been flown, with claims ranging up to and above 1,000 enemy vehicles destroyed or damaged daily. Although the Ninth Air Force night striking force was negligible throughout the war in western Europe, its fighter-bombers achieved limited local success in delaying German movements in darkness by planting delayed-action bombs on key crossroads and choke-points. Attempts were also made to conduct night bombing operations with P–38s by radar control methods, but results were not commensurate with the effort.

During succeeding operations in Normandy and western France it was determined that control efficiency would be immeasurably improved if the tactical air command combat operations and the control group at wing headquarters were placed adjacent to each other. All strike missions of the TAC were initiated at combat operations and much time, personnel and equipment could be saved if combat operations and the fighter control center operated in close physical unity. Immediate decisions could be made and prompt action taken on "hot" targets or targets of opportunity, by having the combat operations officer physically present to make a decision on the diversion of air effort to such targets. In view of these conclusions, after the third move in Normandy the control personnel from both fighters wings in the IX TAC were consolidated into one tactical control group and established physically adjacent to combat operations of the tactical air command. This proved highly efficient and enabled combat operations personnel actually to speak to pilots in flight, giving them first-hand knowledge of the situation, and to direct changes in strike requests. This principle was later adopted by the XIX and XXIX TACs. A direct result of this evolution of fighter control is to be seen in currently approved War Department aircraft control and warning doctrine and in related T/O & Es concerning TACs and the control groups.

A further important development during operations in western France was the realization that the efficiency and effectiveness of operations of the various TACs were almost directly proportionate to the efficiency of their communications and electronic aids. Therefore constant effort was made to improve existing operating procedures for radar equipment, as well as to develop new equipment accessories and new uses for old equipment. Time after time large and lucrative targets of opportunity were spotted by reconnaissance or other fighter aircraft and in a remarkably short time heavy concentrations of aircraft could be assembled to destroy the target. This was possible only through the highly excellent radar communications control network which existed within each tactical air command.

Starting on 1 August the full air-ground program plotted by Supreme Headquarters began to take shape in France. On that day 12th Army Group, Third Army and XIX TAC all became operational on the continent and the Third Army-XIX TAC team went into action with a strike through the St. Lo break-through area to begin the historic "end run through France."

On 5 August Advanced Headquarters, Ninth Air Force, adjacent to and intimately cooperating with 12th Army Group, assumed control of all U. S. tactical air operations and instituted the air force-army group teamwork which was so vital a factor in the success of the entire European campaign. At both air force and TAC level the ground forces established their G–2 Air and G–3 Air staff sections physically within or adjacent to, and intimately cooperating with, the air combat operations section. The two army sections, directly responsible to the Commanding Generals of their own organizations but operating in conjunction with their air force equivalents, furnished the most current army plans, cooperated in screening army requests for tactical air effort and provided valuable target information and ground intelligence not available through air force channels. The establishment of G–2 Air and G–3 Air at air force and TAC headquarters was regarded by air and ground commanders alike as one of the keys to effective air-ground coordination.

With the machinery of joint planning working more smoothly than it ever had before, the air force was prepared to undertake radically new commitments and to achieve, through its inherent flexibility and sensitivity to the ground situation, the most effective and economical employment of its forces. Now that Patton's armor had smashed its way out of the narrow beach-head and Cotentin Peninsula areas and was relatively free to deploy over all of western France against disorganized and spotty resistance, the mobility of the air force, which was evident in the cross-channel movement of tactical units and headquarters, was put to its first severe overland test. XIX TAC's operational headquarters, for example, moved five times during its first month of operation on the continent in order to keep up with the rapidly advancing headquarters of Third Army.

The XIX TAC was given unique responsibilities as Third Army extended the range of its operations to more than 500 miles from Brest in the westernmost part of France to Paris and beyond. The TAC's fighter-bombers simultaneously cooperated in the siege of Brest, gave column cover to armored spearheads racing toward and beyond Paris and, in a bold, unprecedented move, were entrusted by General Patton with full responsibility for guarding the Third Army's long, exposed right flank along the Loire River. The mission of guarding the flank—carried out by vigilant reconnaissance and by fighter-bomber attacks on any masses of German troops which appeared to menace the Third Army "line"—was carried out with such success that the commander of German troops south of the Loire River asked, in negotiations for surrender, that Brig. (later Maj.) Gen. O. P. Weyland, commander of the XIX TAC, be present at the capitulation of the German commander's forces of 20,000 troops on 7 September.

During the German counterattack toward Avranches from Mortain, where the enemy was fanatically determined to force a wedge between the First and Third Armies, IX TAC proved that local air supremacy, which permitted uninterrupted armored column cover and air alert for targets of opportunity over an embattled area, was as effective in denying the enemy any chance of exploiting his ground successes as it was in assuring the success of a properly conceived and planned ground offensive. The IX TAC, assisted by the XIX TAC and a force of British rocket-carrying Typhoons, struck at every suitable target requested by the ground forces, succeeded repeatedly in breaking up powerful German armored and infantry attacks as they were forming and contributed in large part to destroying completely the mobility of the German advance.

The inherent flexibility of the air force was manifested in several ways during the German thrust at Mortain, the closing of the Falaise-Argentan trap and the spectacularly swift advance of the Third Army.

First, airborne fighter-bombers were frequently diverted by the FCC or forward air operations control elements to more opportune or threatening targets, rather than attacking briefed objectives which might have lost their significance even in the short interval between target request and bombing. Secondly, air force reserved sufficient control of operations to be able to shift its full striking force rapidly from one sector to another or even complete tactical units from one TAC's operational control to another's, as the situation demanded. Fighter-bombers of XIX TAC were called in to assist in the primarily IX TAC task of maintaining alerts at Mortain and some IX TAC groups were put under operational control of its sister-command during Third Army's most rapid period of advance. Both TACs and the RAF combined on Germans fleeing from the Falaise pocket in mid-August, destroying many thousands of German vehicles and turning the retreat into a disorderly rout.

The development of the much publicized and greatly feared napalm or "fire bomb" by the Ninth Air Force had reached the stages where "fire bombing" was assuming a role of ever-increasing importance as a weapon against the enemy. Although napalm was never eminently successful, its possibilities were and are great and should be developed.

The headlong withdrawal of the German Seventh and Fifteenth Armies put to the severest test the mobility for which the IX Engineer Command, the IX Air Force Service Command and the IX Air Defense Command had planned, organized and trained. Although it had been expected that transportation facilities would be strained during the period of breakout, the pace of the advance far exceeded anything anticipated. As a result, the tactical disposition of these commands was largely influenced by the day-to-day availability of transport. The air defense command kept its units in close proximity to air units on the move and assumed greater air defense responsibilities in the rear areas. The service command had to move its service units and installations forward with unprecedented rapidity and to move supplies over ever-lengthening and changing lines of communication. Late in August Maj. Gen. Samuel E. Anderson, commanding the IX Bomber Command, continuing without interruption his program of interdiction and destruction of enemy fuel, ammunition, and supply reserves, directed and executed from the United Kingdom the move of four tactical groups to France, in order to extend their range and to permit more frequent bombardment operations by taking advantage of the more favorable weather conditions on the continent.

E. CAMPAIGN OF EASTERN FRANCE AND THE SIEGFRIED LINE (26 August 1944–15 December 1944)

In late August and September the stretching of Allied lines of communication and the stiffening of German resistance at the Siegfried Line slowed the pace of the Allied advance until the battle turned into generally static warfare, which persisted until the German counter-offensive in December.

During this period, in addition to carrying out air operations diminished only because of weather, the Ninth Air Force moved its forces into positions from which they could strike most effectively and at shortest range against the enemy in his homeland.

The capture of large numbers of partially demolished German airfields in the area near and east of Paris made it possible for IX Engineer Command to provide fields not only for air supply and evacuation behind the advance, and for the basing of nearly all fighter and reconnaissance groups east of Laon, but also for the movement of the remaining seven medium bomber groups of IX Bomber Command from England to the Paris area. This latter step had not been contemplated in the pre-invasion planning and was made possible only by the cooperation given by Communications Zone in the provision of more than a proportionate share of rail tonnage for landing mat, bombs, ammunition, and aviation gas. Such provision was endorsed by General Bradley, commanding 12th Army Group, since continued strong air effort was excellent insurance against the enemy marshalling his forces for strong counterattacks.

During the preceding period of rapid advances, when the requirement for airfields became more and more urgent, the engineer command had been hindered considerably by difficulties in moving its vast tonnages of construction supplies into forward areas. Theoretically, other agencies were to assist the command in this transfer of material, but, actually, assistance from outside sources was negligible when it was most urgently required. The engineers, and all other air force commands, would have profited by the establishment of a joint air-ground traffic priority board which determined priorities of movement of personnel and supply.

The period of static warfare gave a sorely needed breathing spell to the air force service command, which by the end of September had improvised lines of communication 600 miles long, from the Normandy beaches to the German frontier, without having had time to establish large dumps which would have simplified the supply channels. At one time the general-purpose-type bomb supply became so low that the TACs had to take careful inventory of all stocks and then divide those stocks among them most equitably. This shortage, however, was not due to service command supply channels but rather to a combination of unforseeable and uncontrollable circumstances. The breathing spell in the autumn of 1944 implied no real rest, for the command had to continue "all-out" preparations for immediate future operations, as well as to restock greatly depleted stocks of bombs, ammunition, equipment, spare parts and other supplies. The supply and movement situation was aggravated by the air force's constant shortage of organic transport; transport was in use 24 hours a day, 7 days a week, allowing no time for maintenance or overhaul. The superlative success of the IX Air Force Service Command in servicing and supplying the great number of air force units must be attributed to Brig. Gen. Myron R. Wood and his staff, who actually put themselves and the entire command on a real and effective 24-hour-a-day, 7-day-a-week basis.

Organizationally the Ninth Air Force in September and October reshaped its functional organization and operating procedure to meet all contingencies which might arise during the assault on the Siegfried Line and the subsequent drive into Germany. In September Main Headquarters moved from the United Kingdom to France and assumed all functions which were not concerned with immediate operations of the air force. The directorate system was adopted, with Brig. Gen. Robert M. Lee as Deputy Commanding General for Operations at Advanced Headquarters and Brig. Gen. Victor H. Strahm as Deputy Commanding General for Administration at Main Headquarters, both directly responsible to Lt. (then Maj.) Gen. Hoyt S. Vandenberg, Commanding General, Ninth Air Force. Discarding the conventional general and special staff system gave general staff status to the Directors of Communications, Reconnaissance, and Weather. The division of the former A–3 section into a Directorate of Combat Operations and a Directorate of Plans and Organization permitted the consolidation of personnel actually engaged in the planning and execution of current operations into a compact combat operations section at Advanced Headquarters. The more static functions of A–3, such as movement, plans and training, were discharged by the Directorate of Plans and Organization at Main Headquarters.

The maintenance of a mobile operational headquarters—relieved of almost all administrative responsibilities—meant that the communications section would have to insure excellent lateral and vertical lines from advanced to co-equal ground headquarters, Main Headquarters and the tactical commands and that, during rapid moves, this system would have to be duplicated at old and new advanced headquarters sites. This was accomplished to such good effect during all phases of the war in western Europe that communications throughout the Ninth Air Force were generally and continuously excellent. It was concluded, however, that the operational channels of communication would have been less crowded if the large flow of operational intelligence reports and messages could have been carried on a separate communications system devoted purely to intelligence usage.

The only definite exception to the general excellence of communications was that the facilities available to the IX ADC were inadequate. Movement liaison failed almost completely because of the lack of land lines. Air warning, intelligence and administrative functions lost about 20 percent efficiency because of the lack of radio and wire communication. Operations suffered to a limited extent. This loss in efficiency would not have occurred if there had been a light construction battalion (signal) assigned to the air defense command.

In late summer of 1944 the air force's operational commitment increased when a third U. S. Army—the Ninth—moved into the line north of the Third and First Armies and the Seventh Army reached positions south of the Third. It was the Ninth Air Force's responsibility to put a tactical air command into operation with the Ninth Army and to be operationally and administratively in control of a fourth TAC during the period when the First Tactical Air Force (Prov) was getting organized for joint operations with the 6th Army Group. XXIX TAC (Prov), commanded by Brig. Gen. Richard E. Nugent, became operational on 2 October, having been organized from elements of the IX and XIX TACs and the virtually dissolved Fighter

Command. XII TAC was administered and controlled by the Ninth Air Force for approximately 6 weeks while First TAF was in process of organization.

The development of the air force in the autumn of 1944 coincided with several improvements in the technique of daylight bombing and night operations, which increased the tactical striking power both of the bombardment force and of the night fighters. Weather experts had estimated that days suitable for unrestricted daylight bombing in Europe would average only about six a month, but the development of instrument bombing, which achieved a high degree of efficiency in the autumn of 1944, permitted the employment of medium bombers in weather which would have been thought prohibitive the previous autumn. Such new and secret equipment as Gee, Shoran, and SCR–584 made bombing through ten-tenths clouds commonplace late in 1944, and medium and light bombers operated on 139 days between 1 October 1944 and 9 May 1945. The frequency and effectiveness of bombardment operations in poor weather was further increased by the work of a weather reconnaissance squadron of P–51 Mustangs, which often arrived in the target area just before the bombers and advised the controllers of weather conditions over the objectives. Instrument bombing units and weather reconnaissance proved indispensable and it is indeed difficult to understand why no provision was made in the original troop basis for either of these types of organization.

In October 1944, in view of the small enemy night effort which practically negated the defensive value of the night fighters, it was decided to transfer the two P–61 night fighter squadrons from the air defense command to the IX and XIX Tactical Air Commands. There they were armed with HVAR rockets, in addition to their 20-mm cannon, and dispatched on offensive night intruder operations as well as primarily defensive night fighter assignments. The excellent results achieved by this small force of night intruder fighters—coupled with the relative freedom from air attack which the Germans enjoyed at night—obviously justified a geometric increase in the size of the night striking force. It was the opinion of the air force that the interdiction program could have been virtually prohibitive for the enemy if night intruder operations had been at all comparable to daylight operations.

The transfer of the night fighter craft from the air defense command discloses the essentially offensive nature of air force operations during the war in western Europe. Initially it was considered that a command responsible for air defense would necessarily posssess aircraft which would be used in a purely defensive role. As the tactical air commands developed increasingly effective means of control of aircraft either by day or night, however, and as the weakness of the German air force and its failure to appear either in force or with any regularity over Allied installations became apparent, it was concluded that it was wasteful to restrict night fighters to defensive operations when the TACs could so much more profitably employ them on intruder missions. Furthermore, the IX ADC by this time had a large and efficient AA component, to which air defense could now be entrusted without fighter aid. It would be improper, however, to draw from this a general conclusion that fighters are unnecessary to an air defense command.

About this time the organization, training and equipping of tactical air parties, which were neglected in the prevailing tables of organization, were proceeding rapidly; as fast as additional parties could be trained they were assigned by the TACs to the armored and infantry corps and divisions in their associated armies. Procedures and techniques for the control of aircraft in flight were perfected and the tactical control centers were completely and elaborately equipped with all the installations necessary for the precise control of airborne aircraft. Communications between tactical reconnaissance planes and fighter control centers or airborne formations were steadily improved until the planes achieved enormous flexibility and the time-lag between mission-request and execution was reduced to minutes.

The air defense command area of responsibility continued to grow as the Allied armies pushed toward the Siegfried Line. By early autumn the command was protecting various air, ground, and naval installations from the beachheads in Normandy all the way to key positions in the rear of army areas in France, Belgium, Holland, and Luxembourg, in addition to guarding all Ninth Air Force operational fields. Under the expert close supervision of Brig. Gen. William L. Richardson, Commanding General of the IX Air Defense Command, a highly efficient defense against buzz-bombs was developed and employed with remarkable effectiveness in the defense of Antwerp, Liege and Brussels against V-bombs.

In mid-October the Germans made a violent effort to prevent Allied use of Antwerp's 30 miles of wharves by launching the most deadly buzz-bomb assault of the war. A special task force, known as Antwerp X, was organized with two AAA brigades from IX Air Defense Command and one British brigade. The success of the task force, which operated under most difficult conditions and which, during the Ardennes break-through, was in part compelled to take up arms as ground soldiers, can best be measured statistically: of 4,883 buzz-bombs launched against Antwerp in 154 days, 2,759 were definitely headed for the port area and 211 got through. In its more orthodox operations against enemy aircraft the air defense command was very successful, although somewhat hampered by recurring misunderstandings which arose between the air and ground forces, due to the insistence by the ground forces that all AAA operating forward of the army rear boundary be under their command.

The variety of aerial operations from September until the German break-through in December was nearly as great as during the preceding period of rapid advances. Heavy, medium, and fighter-bombers were used in the air and ground siege of the permanent forts, heavy pillboxes, and massive inner fortifications of the Siegfried Line and of Brest, with varying effects. Generally speaking, conventional bombardment tactics and weapons were relatively ineffective against such targets and, even when particularly heavy assaults were made, permanent fortifications of modern construction suffered only superficial damage in relation to the required weight of attack.

On 25 September the First Allied Airborne Army executed one of the largest airborne operations of the war in the area of Arnhem, Holland. This extremely difficult and precarious operation was undertaken in an area where the current scale and disposition of antiaircraft defenses were practically unknown. An airborne assault under these conditions was theoretically too dangerous a risk to take. However, General Brereton, with the fullest confidence in the ability of the tactical air forces to eliminate or negate flak and enemy fighter opposition, convinced the Supreme Commander that the operation was feasible. The fact that General Brereton's confidence was not misplaced was completely substantiated by the very small proportion of losses to enemy flak or enemy aircraft sustained by the airborne forces. Gengeneral Brereton subsequently recognized the contribution of the Ninth

Air Force's fighter-bombers in an extremely commendatory message to General Vandenberg, in which he stated that Ninth Air Force fighter-bombers had made a most notable contribution to the success of the operation by their destructive attacks on enemy flak positions.

Fighter-bombers operated more closely to American lines than they ever had before. Of 97 missions flown in cooperation with the 2nd Infantry Division after 23 August at least 65 percent were at the request of front-line battalions or forward observers. Fighter-bombing attacks were particularly effective in silencing enemy artillery, destroying supplies, ammunition, and POL and immobilizing vehicular and armored traffic within the German area. The dispatch of fighter-bombers on armed reconnaissance missions not only reduced all German movement to a minimum but such airborne missions were normally available for the execution of close-in cooperation missions when they were required. However, Phase 3 operations in close cooperation with the ground forces decreased as the front became static and the ground forces were able to bring up their own artillery to strike at enemy installations in the front line area.

During static warfare the tactical air force was preoccupied chiefly with Phase 2 operations to prevent the Germans from using these periods to build up and reinforce their front line positions. Medium bombers executed precision attacks against larger German communications centers in the rear and attempted to obliterate stores of ammunition, fuel, and supplies which the enemy accumulated behind the front. Fighter-bombers continued the interception of reserves and supplies on roads and railway lines leading up to the battle area. A modified form of armored column cover was employed, as leaders of fighter-bomber formations checked in with forward ground control posts to determine whether any attacks on Phase 3 targets were required before proceeding on armed reconnaissance against German transport and rear area installations. Much experimental overcast bombing and instrument bombing was done with SCR–584 in an effort to develop and employ efficiently this means of radar control.

Exceptions to this general emphasis on Phase 1 and 2 operations occurred occasionally during the months before the German counteroffensive. Particular examples were: the drive from the west toward the Roer River, where fighter-bombers were employed against the perimeter of German village defenses supporting larger towns; the 12-

day campaign against Aachen, where all types of aircraft were used in a sustained aerial assault against the entrenched enemy; in river campaigns, such as the crossing of the Moselle, where fighter-bombers assured the successful consolidation and expansion of the bridgehead by intercepting and disrupting enemy efforts to bring up reserves; in close-in operations on the bridgehead front and in larger operations, such as MADISON at Metz and QUEEN near Eschweiler, where bombers carpeted entire defended areas and fighter-bombers protected the flanks and front of the attacking ground forces.

Throughout operations on the continent Headquarters Ninth Air Force seldom attempted to conduct detailed tactical planning for air-ground thrusts. Such planning was almost invariably done by the TACs in close coordination with Army plans. Normally only over-all objectives were prescribed by air force. Immediate application of air power was planned at TAC level.

The ground forces sometimes made unusual requests for air attack. The request made by the XII Army Corps to the XIX TAC to breach the Dieuze dam east of Nancy, France, during the static period on the Third Army front late in October proved to be a major achievement for fighter-bombers. The request was made to prevent the Germans from blowing the dam and flooding the army's lines of communications along the Seille River when it launched its offensive on 8 November. Because precise pinpoint bombing was required, P–47s were employed instead of medium and heavy bombers. One 1,000-pound bomb breached the dam and the resultant flood was controlled by Army engineers. So successful was the flooding that XII Corps was ready for the offensive on 8 November. It was the first time in the European theater that fighter-bombers were assigned such a mission.

During the rapid advance in August it was impossible (and would have been superfluous) for photographic reconnaissance to attempt a complete basic coverage of enemy terrain; instead, the planes photographed the principal routes of advance and flew "strips" along major terrain obstacles, such as the Meuse, Moselle, Saar, and Rhine Rivers. With the slow-up in September, however, photographic reconnaissance instituted and completed basic coverage of the entire area immediately ahead of the armies, with extremely beneficial results for both ground and air forces. Tactical reconnaissance aircraft, meanwhile, explored the German lines of communication, reported their findings to the fighter control center and often guided fighter-bombers to targets which otherwise might have remained unsighted and undisturbed. A further employment of Tac/R planes was in the conduct of artillery adjustment when the selected target was too dangerously far behind the lines for the slow and vulnerable liaison-type artillery reconnaissance aircraft.

The increased volume of reconnaissance during the static period, in which ground commanders seldom had to move without detailed and recent photographs of the area ahead to guide them, was technically supervised and coordinated by the new Directorate of Photography and Reconnaissance established in air force headquarters early in September. The Ninth Air Force's own facilities for reproduction, printing, and interpretation were extremely inadequate throughout the war and considerable use had to be made of the Eighth Air Force's more extensive and better equipped static installations for processing photographs which were not in immediate operational demand, such as mapping photography, semi-strategic target material, etc.

The attempt by IX Engineer Command to provide bases for all tactical groups of the three TACs close behind the rapidly stabilizing front, in preparation for a later offensive, was defeated by the onset of the autumn rains in late September. Had the weather held for another week or 10 days most of the new fields in the Liege, Metz, and Nancy areas could have been completed with Hessian surfacing and the air force would have been poised close behind the lines, ready to resume the offensive at any time through the winter. In the event that the rains were so protracted and of such unprecedented severity that the fields under construction were soon mud-bound, it would be necessary to settle down to deliberate construction of rock subgrades, involving hundreds of thousands of cubic yards of rock fill and millions of truck-miles. In the course of this heavy construction effort, under the most atrocious conditions of mud and ice, the lack of supporting dump-truck companies and Ordnance maintenance companies led to such a deterioration of the aviation engineer's organic transportation as almost to destroy the mobility of the engineer command, and thus of the air force.

F. CAMPAIGN OF THE ARDENNES (16 December 1944–28 January 1945)

In mid-December 12th Army Group was poised for two powerful assaults on the Siegfried Line, the major one in the north with the lower Rhine as its objective, the lesser one in the south directed toward the Saar and the Palatinate. The ground forces were aware during this period that the Germans were building up strength and that a counteroffensive was possible. The general opinion, however, was that the German effort would be an attempt to eliminate the American salient, which included the city of Aachen and the territory to the south, where the two dams which controlled the flood stage of the Roer River were menaced by slow but steady American advances.

Carefully timing the jump-off to coincide with a period of poor weather which would hamper Allied reconnaissance and prohibit full use of tactical air power von Runstedt on 16 December launched a major offensive with the object of isolating the Allied armies east of Liege, Brussels, and Antwerp and relieving the intolerable pressure which these forces were exerting against the Siegfried Line. The extended period of poor weather prior to the attack, with consequent freedom from aerial reconnaissance observation, an admittedly marked degree of surprise—not at the attack, but at its massive scale—and the thinness of American troops in position to resist the German advance, gave the enemy counteroffensive a strong initial impact. Further to exploit this advantage the GAF put forth its strongest effort of the war, concentrating from 500 to 600 aircraft a day in the battle zone, more than twice the number which ordinarily appeared daily over the entire front.

During the first 2 days of the break-through the weather was flyable and violent battles were fought between the GAF and the Ninth. More than 145 enemy planes were destroyed in the air on these 2 days alone, but on 18 December poor weather forced a lull in Ninth Air Force operations which lasted 5 days and during which scarcely more than 200 sorties were flown daily. Although fighter-bombers were compelled to fly at hazardously low altitudes under extremely poor weather conditions and severely limited visibility, they made an invaluable contribution to the ground effort by blunting a major enemy armored thrust toward Stavelot and the immense and relatively undefended fuel stores beyond the town.

Although the daylight hours up to 23 December were characterized by low, icy clouds, the nights were clear and the inadequacy of the night striking force of the Ninth Air Force was never so clearly revealed as it was at this critical time. The Germans were practically free to make any movements they wished at night or in the daytime.

The initial surprise and effectiveness of the enemy attack put the air force on the defensive for the first time and again tested its flexibility. Advanced Headquarters at Luxembourg maintained its close supervisory control of operations, although the town was under shell fire from German artillery only a few miles away and although direct lines to IX and XXIX TACs in the north were severed or compromised. Furthermore, the general division of the Allied forces made it imperative that the First and Ninth Armies be shifted to the operational control of the British 21st Army Group. Consequently IX and XXIX TACs were temporarily transferred to the operational control of the British Second TAF, which was the air partner of the 21st Army Group. To avoid an inequitable distribution of tactical air power between the northern and southern ends of the enemy salient the air force transferred three fighter-bomber groups to the XIX TAC from the commands to the north. In addition, two fighter groups from the Eighth Air Force were brought to the continent and placed under the control of the Ninth, releasing the Ninth's fighter-bombers from air defense commitments and increasing the available effort against German ground forces. Further to strengthen the tactical air forces the entire 2nd Division of the Eighth Air Force was placed under the operational control of the Ninth Air Force. Air power was to smother completely Germany's greatest tactical air effort of the war in western Europe in 2 days, with fearful losses to the enemy.

General Eisenhower's strategy was to destroy the power of the counter-offensive at its source by heavy incessant interdiction from the air, while containing the attacking elements within a limited and predefined area. The role of bombers of the Eighth and Ninth Air Forces was to attack railway yards, communications centers, and bridges along two concentric lines of interdiction east of the base of the salient. The object of this program was to deny mobility to the army within the bulge, to restrict the enemy's flexibility of operations and to sever all lines of communication and supply. The role of fighter-bombers was to insure the success of the interdiction program by extensive Phase 1 and 2 operations initially and then, once air supremacy had definitely been re-established, gradually to build up the volume of Phase 3 operations at the expense of Phase 1.

The accomplishment of this program began on 23 December, when, to quote a hard-pressed doughboy, "the war's most beautiful sunrise" ushered in the first of a series of 5 clear operational days, permitting the Ninth Air Force to bring its full power to bear against the counter-offensive. The 9th Bombardment Division immediately launched a carefully planned campaign of rail and road interdiction within and east of the salient, frequently delaying even minor movement of enemy combat units for 24 hours or more. As these operations continued, the enemy was compelled gradually to shift his railheads supporting the counter-offensive back to the Rhine and to try to make fuller use of the road net east of the Ardennes. However, there the fighter-bombers relentlessly hunted the highways for German motor and armored transport, almost completely forcing it off the roads in daylight hours. The enemy's acute shortage of gasoline, one of the decisive reasons for the failure of his counter-offensive, was further aggravated by these effective road-hunting operations. The 5 good flying days up to 28 December, when weather closed in again temporarily, resulted in a serious throttling of the enemy's flow of supplies and reserves and virtually put an end to German hopes of isolating the Allied combat armies to the north.

Meanwhile, at Bastogne, fighter-bombers cooperated with the beleaguered 101st Division by attacking close-in targets which could not have been hit by American artillery because of a critical shortage of ammunition. Supply by air, with a good percentage of recovery, sustained the defensive during the most difficult days at Bastogne. Night fighter intruder operations against harassing Luftwaffe forces were effective as far as they could go, but the inadequacy of the night force was sharply felt, as always.

The enemy air effort reached its peak on 1 January, when the Luftwaffe dispatched approximately 600 aircraft in an early morning attack against forward airfields in both the British and the American zones. More than 50 percent of the attacking force was destroyed as fighter-bombers and antiaircraft units combined in their most effective counter-air force teamwork of the war. Severe, destructive attacks on several Ninth Air Force bases were unsuccessful in their primary purpose of reducing, delaying, or suspending aerial operations, for within 24 hours sufficient replacement aircraft arrived from service command depots to maintain normal operations without diminution or interruption. Admittedly, however, the task of replacing these aircraft so swiftly put a strain on the service command's supply line. The German air effort also failed to delay the recuperation of American ground forces after the initial break-through and 12th Army Group concluded after the battle of the Ardennes that the Luftwaffe had had only a nuisance effect on American infantry and armored forces.

As early as 31 December fighter-bombers of the Ninth Air Force, some of which were operating from newly completed airfields in the vicinity of Metz and Maastricht, were cooperating intimately with the ground forces in a new offensive to drive the Germans out of their area of penetration. Practically cut off from their supply sources, driven from the roads in the daylight and bombed incessantly in villages within the salient, the enemy forces soon decided to retreat to prepared defensive positions rather than to try to maintain the tenuously held captured area. Although this retreat never turned into a rout it was grossly expensive for the enemy, since fighter-bombers destroyed thousands of vehicles on the various main and secondary roads leading out of the bulge. In one particularly well-coordinated air force operation medium bombers on 22 January destroyed a bridge crossing the Our River at Dasburg and caused an enormous traffic jam on the west bank of the river. Fighter-bombers, attacking continuously until darkness, destroyed or damaged that day alone almost 3,000 motor and armored vehicles among the concentrations created by the bridge attack. By the end of January all ground lost in the counter-offensive had been recovered by the American ground forces.

G. CAMPAIGN WEST OF THE RHINE RIVER (29 January 1945–24 March 1945)

After the threat in the Ardennes had been eliminated the First and Third Armies resumed their drive toward the Rhine. All three phases of the tactical mission were discharged by the tactical air commands, although the proportion of Phase 3 missions fell slightly below the average for the period from August to January. The IX TAC continued to cooperate with the First Army in the comparatively slow drive to the western banks of the Roer. Fighter-bombers of XIX Tactical Air Command, frequently striking within sight of the front lines as the Third Army crossed the Prum, the Saar and the Moselle, helped form and reduce enemy pockets in the 130-square-mile area of the Moselle-Saar triangle guarding the approaches to Trier.

Farther north the formation of a huge new pocket was begun by a series of planned attacks on key communications points around the perimeter of the Ruhr Valley. This interdiction campaign, one of the most important preoccupations of the Ninth Air Force during February and March, was carried out largely by medium and light bombers, while fighter-bombers flew mostly against moving vehicles on railway lines and roads approaching the Ruhr from the east, north, and south. One of the most remarkable phases of the general interdiction campaign came on 22 February 1945, when all available Allied aircraft combined in Operation CLARION, a series of simultaneous attacks designed to paralyze the entire railway system in western Germany, with particular emphasis on the areas east of the Ruhr, east of Coblenz, and in the Palatinate. The planning and execution of the Ninth Air Force part of this massive assault were superb and resulted in one of its most successful days of operations during the entire war. As its share in the total operation 9th Bombardment Division divided its bombers into small formations, which struck at 61 bridges, junctions, sidings, and railway yards. Forty-one of these formations dropped to low levels after the bombing, to strafe German targets of opportunity on the roads and railway lines. This operation and subsequent operations insured that the German railway system in the Ninth Air Force sector of responsibility was of little use to the Wehrmacht.

On 23 February, coordinating their air assault with the ground troops which were launching a heavy attack across the Roer River, medium and light bombers were effectively employed against communications centers and railway yards and contributed materially to the inability of the enemy to marshal his forces effectively for a counter-attack or for a coherent defense. Attacks on fortified towns in connection with the Roer crossings also had good effect and resulted in restriction of the enemy's use of artillery against the crossings. Fighter-bombers carried out particularly active Phase 2 and 3 operations throughout the period of this offensive, literally withering enemy attempts to set up road blocks and maintain defensive stands. Fighter-bombers attacked with everything they had, including fire bombs, H. E. bombs, fragmentation clusters, rockets, and eight 50-caliber machine guns. Another contribution of these aircraft was to permit troops to concentrate for the jump-off without interference from enemy air.

On 2 March the First Army reached the Rhine and soon after crossed the Ludendorf bridge at Remagen and swiftly established a bridgehead east of the Rhine. Fighter-bombers by this time were experienced in the defense of precarious bridgeheads and when the Germans pitted ME–262s, JU–87s and heavy artillery against First Army elements on the eastern bank of the Rhine IX TAC immediately established an air patrol over the area, to cooperate with massed antiaircraft responsible for the close air defense of the bridge. Meanwhile other fighter-bombers swept ahead to attack all possible bases from which Germans were taking off against the bridgehead. A typical attack was against the Lippe airfield on 15 March, which resulted in the destruction or damaging of more than 100 enemy aircraft on the ground. As a further safeguard to the preservation of this all-important bridgehead First Army and IX TAC transmitted a request to air force-army group headquarters that medium bombers carry out an interdiction campaign against railway targets which might support German forces in the bridgehead area. These operations, most of them carried out by instrument bombing through heavy clouds, helped weaken enemy opposition to the First Army and minimized the movement of German reserves to the critical area.

The second Rhine crossing was made easily and speedily by the Third Army on the night of 22 March. The following morning fighter-bombers of XIX TAC initiated the usual program of area cover and direct cooperation and kept in the air from first light to dusk. A number of German planes were shot down when the Luftwaffe attempted a slight revival of its aerial campaign against the Third Army. However, fighter-bombers were primarily useful against German gun positions, troop concentrations, command installations, and vehicles. Toward the end of March the battleground was rapidly shifting east of the Rhine to the heart of Germany and eastward to Czechoslovakia and Austria.

On 19 March, during this campaign, fighter-bombers of the XIX TAC were sent to destroy the headquarters of the German Commander-in-Chief, West, at Ziegenburg, near Bad Nauheim. This old castle, where Hitler and von Runstedt planned the Ardennes break-through, was attacked by P–47s during the noon meal hour, from minimum altitudes. The 1,000- and 500-pound GP and 150-gallon napalm fire bombs launched by two squadrons put the entire headquarters, including the castle and adjacent buildings, out of any future use. General von Runstedt, following his capture, complained: "Allied planes not only shattered our supply lines but they carried the war right home by hitting the headquarters at Bad Nauheim."

H. CAMPAIGN OF CENTRAL GERMANY, AUSTRIA AND CZECHOSLOVAKIA (25 March 1945–7 May 1945)

The third Rhine crossing was made by two airborne divisions of the First Allied Airborne Army, which were dropped in the Wesel area on 23 March 1945 as fighter-bombers flew thousands of sorties against German flak positions in the drop zones and protected the long procession of tugs and gliders. Not one plane of any description was lost to air attack during the airborne crossing—an indication both of the effectiveness of the escort and of the success of recent attacks on ME–262 jet and other airfields by the Eighth and Ninth Air Forces and the RAF.

With three Rhine bridgeheads at widely separated points the immobile and shattered German army was unable to put up any effective resistance and Allied ground forces made swift progress on all fronts. The Ninth and First Armies closed the Ruhr pocket on 1 April, some time after the great industrial valley had been rendered practically useless to the enemy because of the disorganization of the entire German transportation system. Air assisted in reducing stubborn enemy elements within the pocket, as fighter-bombers paced the Ninth Army break-through in which some ground units gained 200 miles in 2 weeks. Fighter-bombers flew principally armored column cover, closely co-ordinating air attacks with ground effort, enabling the attacking forces speedily to reduce road blocks, overcome strongpoints and occupy defended buildings and field fortifications. Defensively, the same planes flew protective patrols which were particularly important during build-up stages when heavy concentrations of Allied armor were vulnerable to air attack. Tactical reconnaissance aircraft informed forward ground units of the location of demolished bridges and of resistance pockets until Ninth Army reached the west bank of the Elbe as the Russians arrived on the east bank.

During this period the combined American air forces added the final touches to the destruction of the German Air Force, which by this time was concentrated on relatively few airfields and was almost completely grounded by the critical fuel shortage. In one 7-day period the Eighth, Ninth and First Tactical Air Forces destroyed or damaged more than 3,400 enemy aircraft on the ground.

Toward the end of April IX and XXIX Tactical Air Commands virtually ceased operation, as they received instructions to fly only reconnaissance and defensive patrols. At this time an agreement was reached with the Russians that the depth of American fighter-bomber operations would be limited to the western bank of the Elbe River, although our aircraft had a much longer range and could easily have attacked targets in the Berlin area and beyond. Because of these restrictions, which were dictated by the fluidity and confusion of the battle on the eastern front, few important operations were executed by the IX and XXIX TACs in the last month of the campaign. One exception was a series of attacks off the coast near Flensburg, where it was believed German government officials and military leaders were seeking to escape to Norway. XIX TAC, meanwhile, turned southward with Third Army toward the supposed national redoubt area in the Bavarian Alps and continued close cooperation and armed reconnaissance operations after the tactical air war had to all intents and purposes ended in the north. Fighter-bombers of the TAC chased and shot up columns of Germans moving southward, led ground columns in races to aid the Wehrmacht in protecting prisoners against the more lawless German elements and smashed any concentrations of German troops they were able to find. Groups from each of the other two TACs were transferred to the operational control of the XIX Tactical Air Command during this period to assist in the air campaign against German movement toward the redoubt. By the first part of May there was nothing further for the Ninth Air Force to attack and several days before VE-day the air force ceased offensive operations altogether.

It had been apparent since the tactical groups had been more or less equally apportioned among the TACs, that fighter wing headquarters, in modern tactical air war, were more parasitic than productive. Each TAC, during the major portion of operations on the continent, rarely controlled more than six fighter groups and found that it could more efficiently control and administer them directly.

Thus the wing headquarters became both administratively and, in view of the early relocation and reassignment of their operational control element to the TAC headquarters, operationally surplus. In fact they were reduced to the status of mere switchboards for the reception and transmission of combat information.

It is felt most important to mention here that, during the entire operational period of the Ninth Air Force, there was never an adequate means of front-line demarcation. These existed then and there exists now an urgent requirement for some type of electronic device which can insure the safety of friendly troops during close-in air bombardment.

In the final days of the war many Ninth Air Force tactical, service, and headquarters units began preparing for redeployment. It became increasingly obvious as early as the middle of April that Germany was utterly defeated. Therefore units scheduled for early redeployment to the Pacific were "stood down" from operations and began training, packing, and crating records and equipment in order to expedite their transfer to the Pacific.

Second only to redeployment in priority was the air disarmament program undertaken by the air disarmament command which operated under the IX Air Force Service Command. Huge air disarmament centers were established at Hanau, Frankfurt, just off the Augsburg-Munich autobahn, etc. The air disarmament program, which had begun in the autumn of 1944 with the overrunning of German air bases and installations in France, was just swinging into full stride as Germany finally surrendered unconditionally and all hostilities officially ceased.

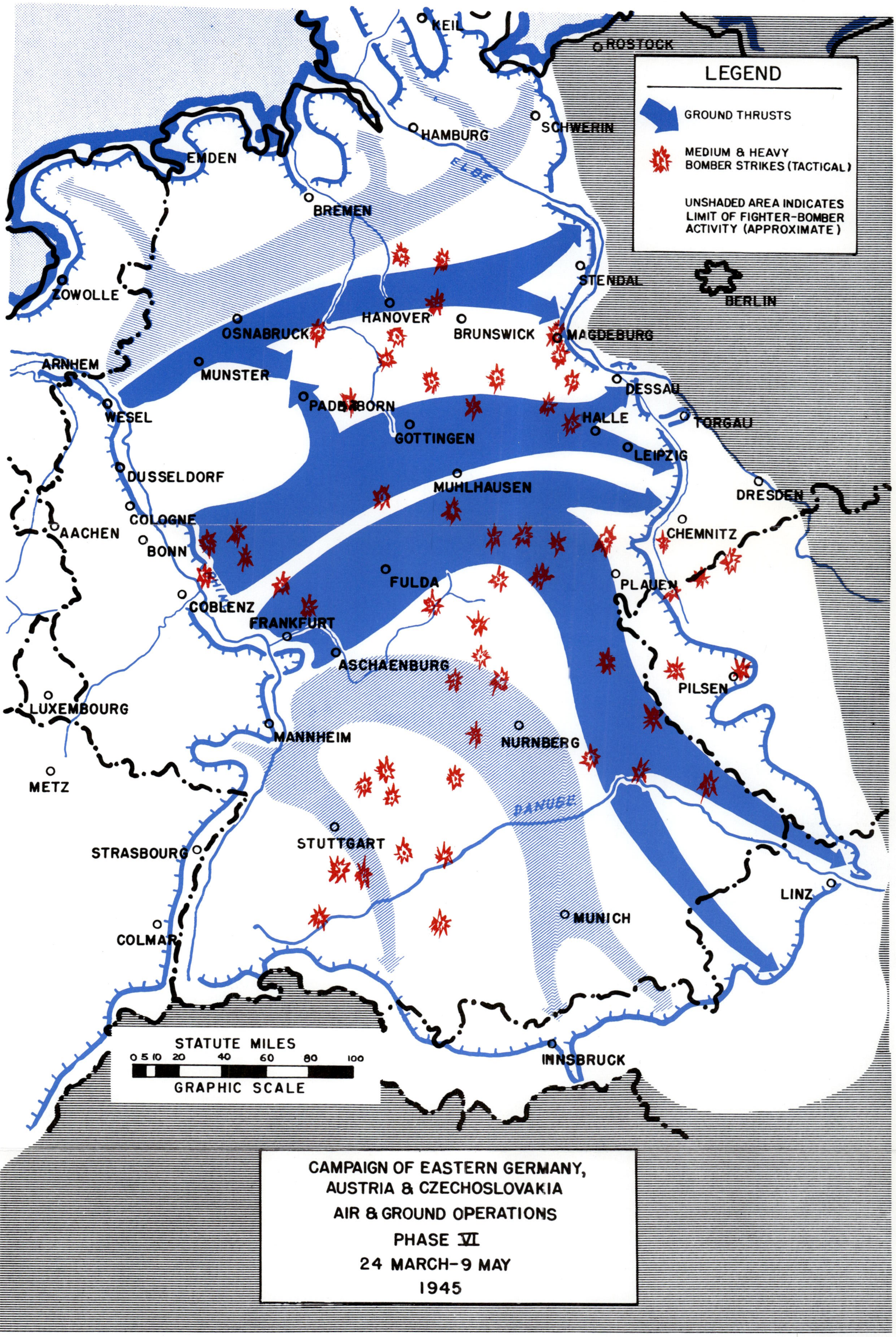

CAMPAIGN OF EASTERN GERMANY,
AUSTRIA & CZECHOSLOVAKIA
AIR & GROUND OPERATIONS
PHASE VI
24 MARCH–9 MAY
1945

682305 O - 46 (Face p. 48) No. 6

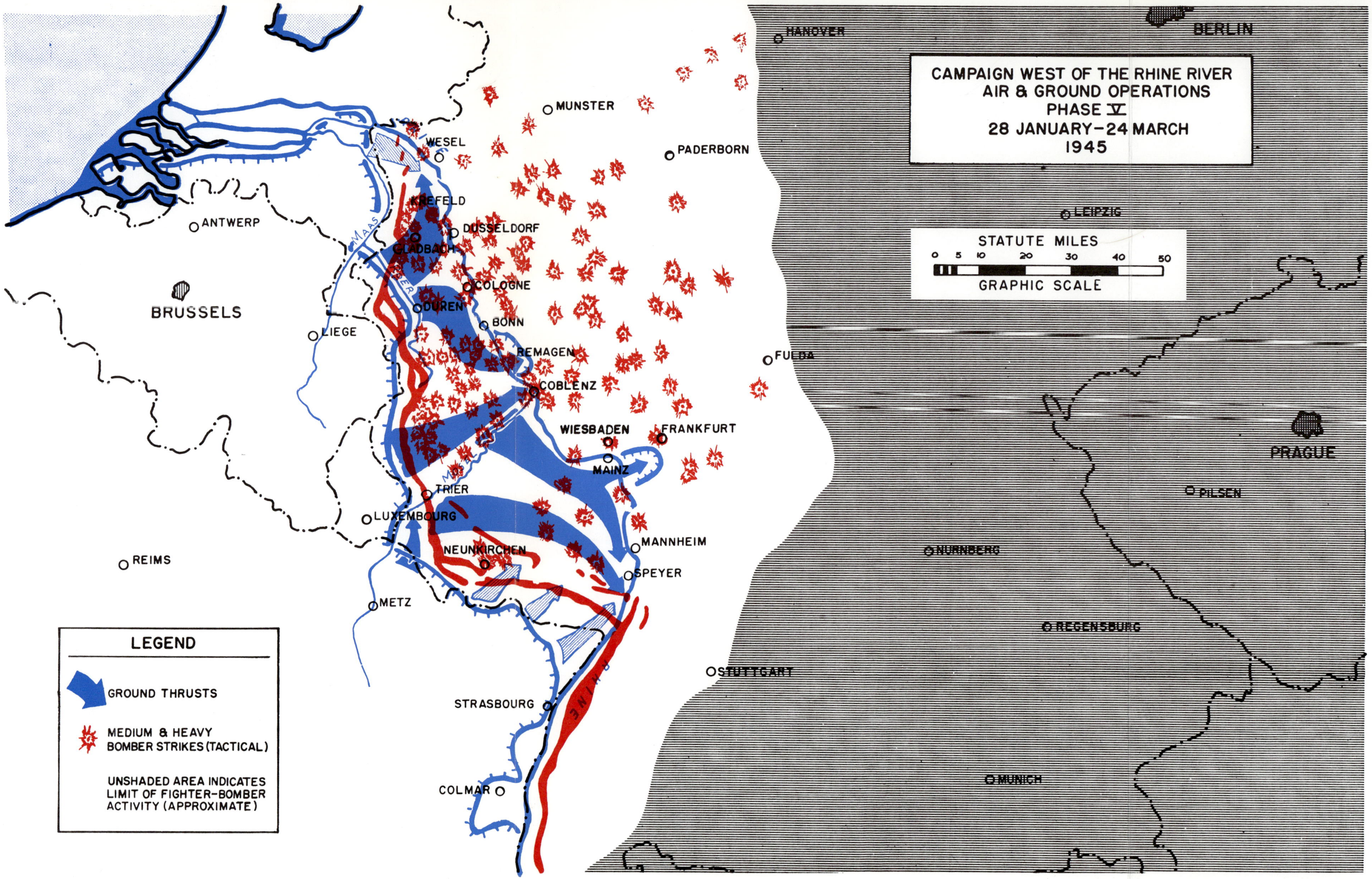
CAMPAIGN WEST OF THE RHINE RIVER
AIR & GROUND OPERATIONS
PHASE V
28 JANUARY–24 MARCH
1945
LEGEND
GROUND THRUSTS
MEDIUM & HEAVY BOMBER STRIKES (TACTICAL)
UNSHADED AREA INDICATES LIMIT OF FIGHTER-BOMBER ACTIVITY (APPROXIMATE)
STATUTE MILES
0 5 10 20 30 40 50
GRAPHIC SCALE
HANOVER
BERLIN
MUNSTER
WESEL
PADERBORN
KREFELD
DUSSELDORF
GLADBACH
ANTWERP
MAAS
LEIPZIG
COLOGNE
DUREN
BRUSSELS
BONN
LIEGE
REMAGEN
FULDA
COBLENZ
WIESBADEN
FRANKFURT
MAINZ
PRAGUE
TRIER
PILSEN
LUXEMBOURG
MANNHEIM
REIMS
NEUNKIRCHEN
NURNBERG
SPEYER
METZ
REGENSBURG
STUTTGART
STRASBOURG
RHINE
MUNICH
COLMAR

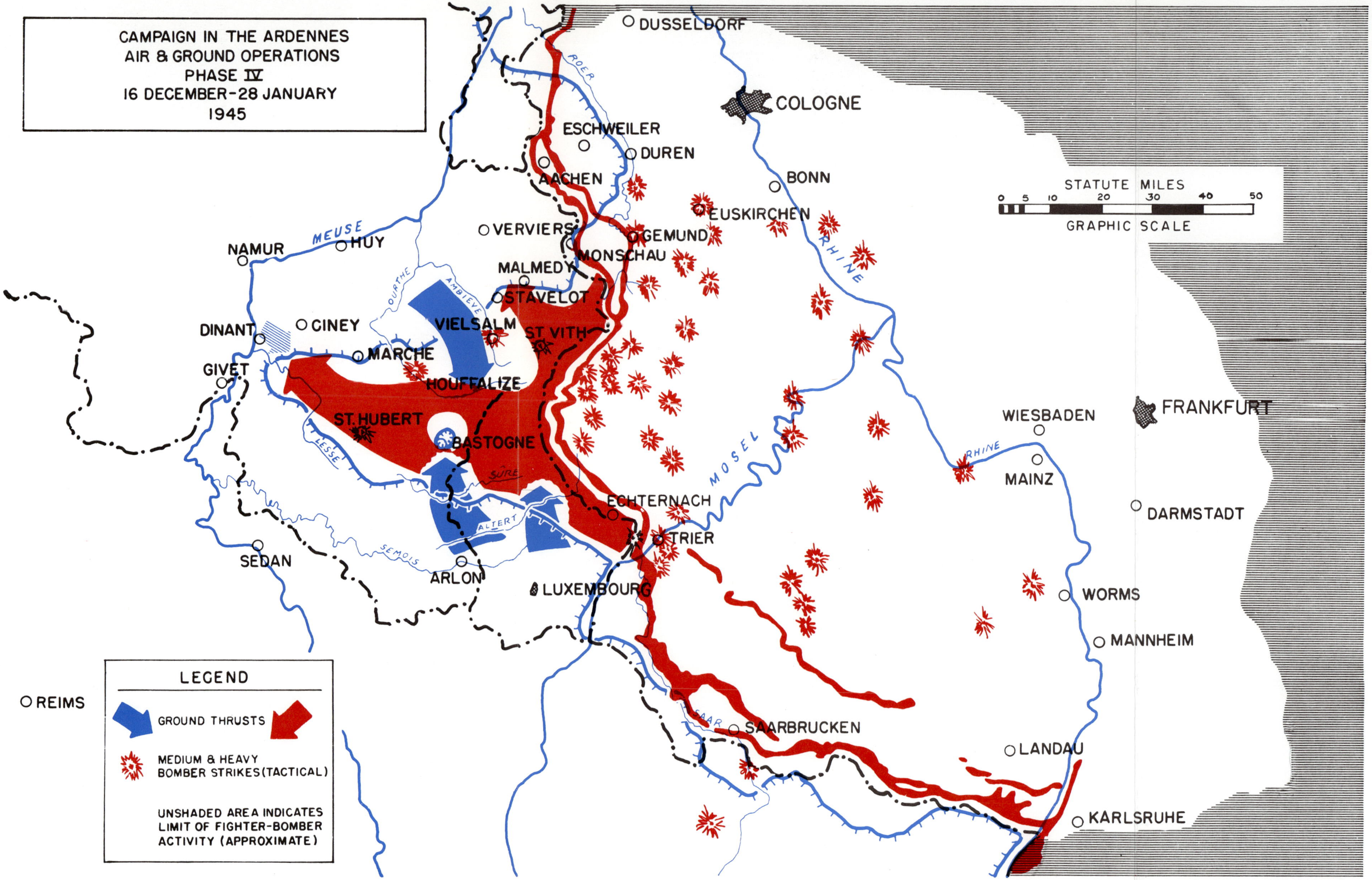

682305 O - 46 (Face p. 48) No. 4

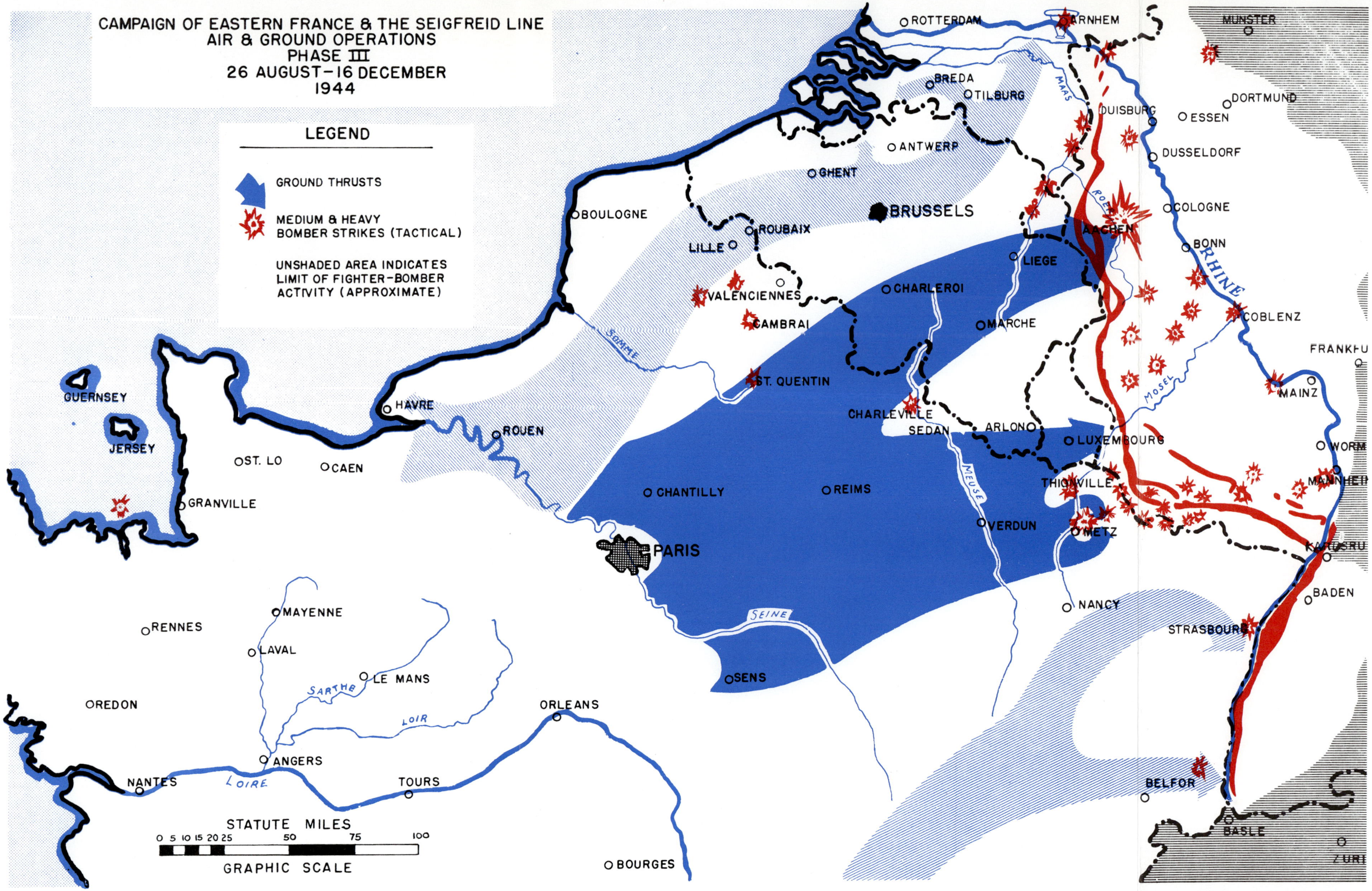

682305 O - 46 (Face p. 48) No. 3

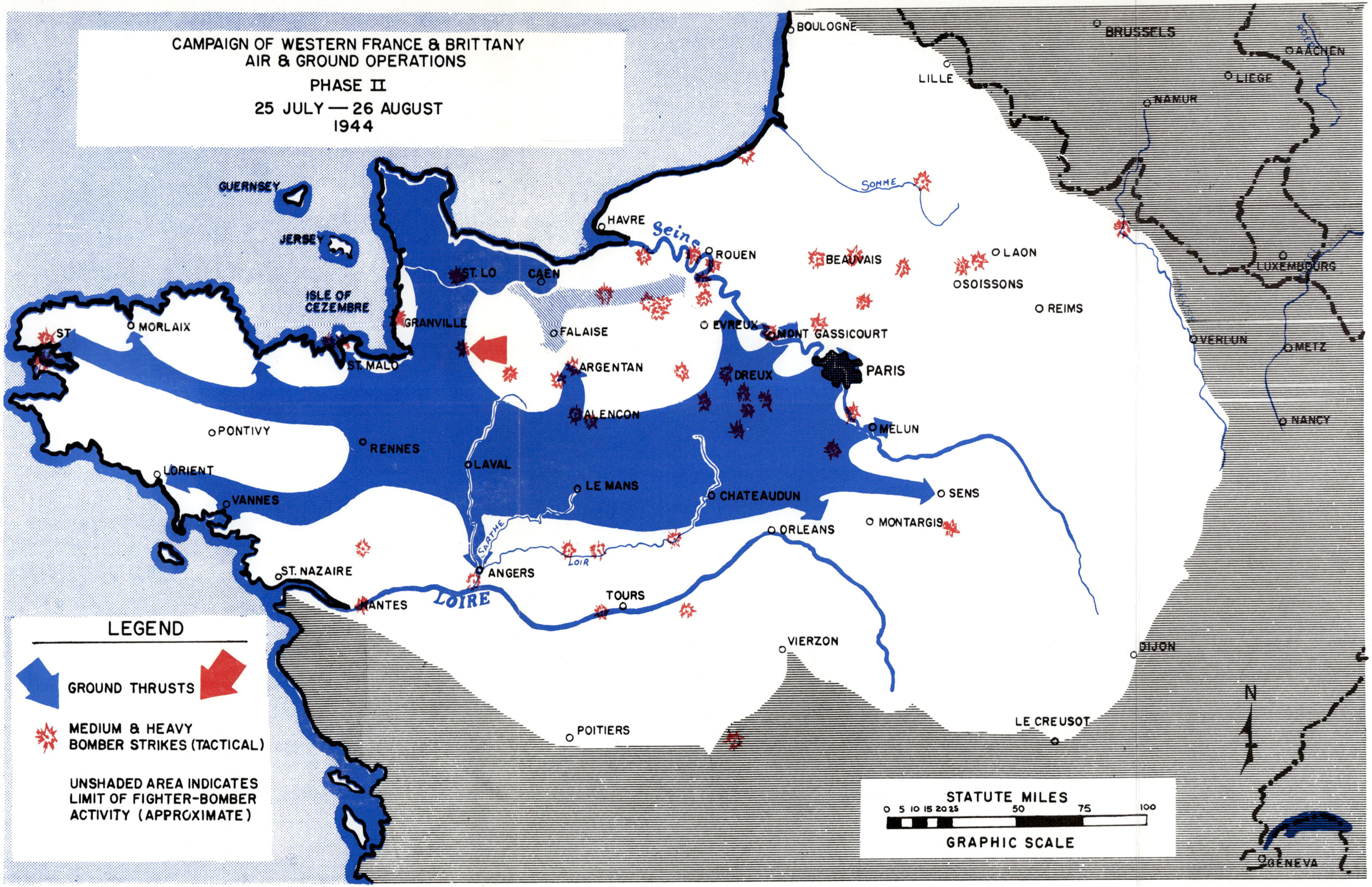

682305 O - 46 (Face p. 48) No. 2

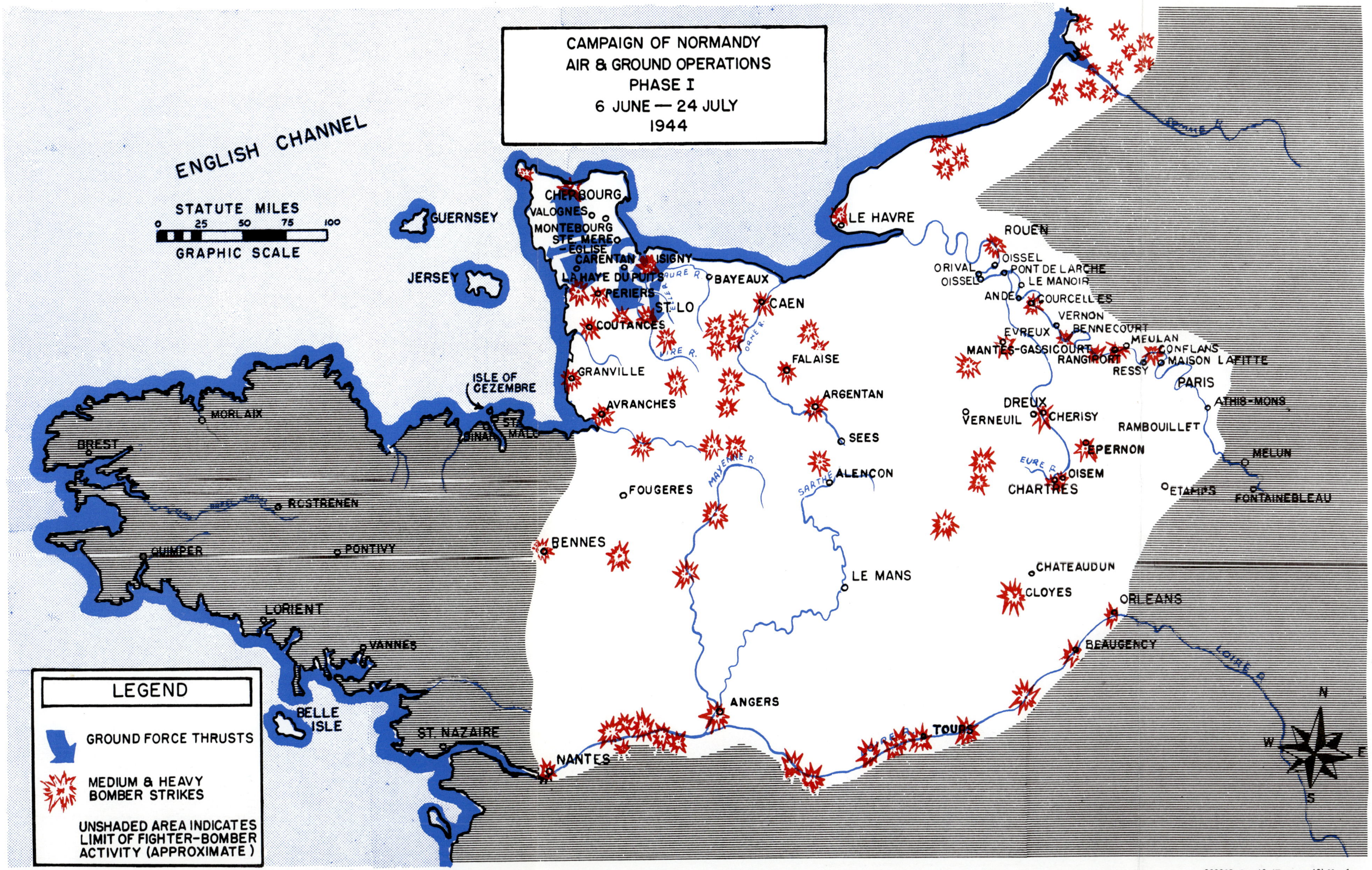

CAMPAIGN OF NORMANDY
AIR & GROUND OPERATIONS
PHASE I
6 JUNE — 24 JULY
1944
ENGLISH CHANNEL
STATUTE MILES
0 25 50 75 100
GRAPHIC SCALE
GUERNSEY
JERSEY
CHERBOURG
VALOGNES
MONTEBOURG
STE MERE-EGLISE
CARENTAN
ISIGNY
LA HAYE DU PUITS
PERIERS
BAYEAUX
ST LO
COUTANCES
CAEN
LE HAVRE
ROUEN
FALAISE
ARGENTAN
SEES
ALENCON
GRANVILLE
AVRANCHES
ISLE OF CEZEMBRE
ST MALO
DINAN
MORLAIX
BREST
ROSTRENEN
QUIMPER
PONTIVY
LORIENT
VANNES
BELLE ISLE
ST NAZAIRE
NANTES
RENNES
FOUGERES
LE MANS
ANGERS
TOURS
ORIVAL
OISSEL
PONT DE LARCHE
LE MANOIR
ANDE
COURCELLES
VERNON
BENNECOURT
EVREUX
MANTES-GASSICOURT
RANGIPORT
MEULAN
CONFLANS
MAISON LAFITTE
RESSY
PARIS
ATHIS-MONS
DREUX
VERNEUIL
CHERISY
RAMBOUILLET
EPERNON
OISEM
CHARTRES
MELUN
ETAMPS
FONTAINEBLEAU
CHATEAUDUN
CLOYES
ORLEANS
BEAUGENCY
VIRE R.
ORNE R.
MAYENNE R
SARTHE R
EURE R
LOIRE R
SOMME R
N
S
E
W
LEGEND
GROUND FORCE THRUSTS
MEDIUM & HEAVY BOMBER STRIKES
UNSHADED AREA INDICATES LIMIT OF FIGHTER-BOMBER ACTIVITY (APPROXIMATE)

Chapter III

A CRITICAL REVIEW OF NINTH AIR FORCE ORGANIZATION

A. ORGANIZATION AND BUILD-UP

EARLY IN 1943 the Army Air Forces began intensive planning for a tactical air component of great striking power, which would be organized in Britain to cooperate with the ground and naval forces assembling for the invasion of Europe. These plans took perhaps their first concrete form in a combined bomber offensive scheme submitted by the Eighth Air Force to the Combined Chiefs of Staff in Washington and calling for a vast expansion of the tactical, technical, administrative, and service components of the Eighth. The plan was that the enlarged, versatile air force would ultimately divide into a strategic half and a tactical half, each of which would concentrate upon its own type of operation but would complement the other's effort whenever necessary. The tactical component would initially be placed under the VIII Air Support Command but would probably be converted into an Eighth Tactical Air Force when it reached full strength. As an indication of the size of the tactical component the Eighth Air Force proposed tentatively that its tactical units include 9 medium bombardment groups, 11 light bombardment groups, 6 dive bombardment groups and 9 troop-carrier groups.

The immediate reaction at Headquarters, Army Air Forces, to the Eighth Air Force's proposals was to send a fact-finding, planning commission of officers under Maj. Gen. Follet Bradley to Britain to study the requirements of the air force there and to prepare recommendations for expansion. The report (the Bradley Plan), submitted to the War Department late in May through the Eighth Air Force and ETOUSA, still envisioned an Eighth Tactical Air Force but in other respects recommended an organization remarkably similar to the Ninth Air Force as it was finally constituted. In particular the Bradley commission recognized that tactical aviation would at first operate from fixed bases but would later move to the continent to operate with the ground forces there.

A further contribution to tactical air force planning was made by Lt. Gen. Jacob C. Devers, then theater commander, who said in his indorsement to the Bradley Plan that the future troop basis would recommend a reduction in the number of medium bombardment groups and a corresponding increase in fighter-bomber groups. The Bradley Plan, with the Devers amendments, was studied in Washington for almost 2 months, but in the interval the Combined Chiefs of Staff, Supreme Allied Command, forerunner of SHAEF, apparently assumed that the plan as amended had been accepted as the blueprint for U. S. tactical air development in Britain.

The AAF branch of COSSAC and Eighth Air Force each prepared a prospective troop basis for the new tactical air force, the former to include more than 175,000 men, the latter more than 200,000 in 3 air support commands, a troop carrier command, an air service command, and an air force headquarters.

The War Department, however, returned the Bradley Plan to the theater with a list of significant exceptions, with which the commander of the Eighth Air Force strongly disagreed. To resolve the points of dispute Headquarters AAF instructed Col. James W. Baylor and a group of experts to proceed to the ETO to mediate the question of AAF requirements and to request approval for whatever adjustments were considered necessary. Colonel Baylor urged the adoption of the Bradley Plan without fundamental change and recommended acceleration of the movement of air force units to Britain.

Meanwhile—to complete this sketch of the intricate planning background of the Ninth Air Force—the commander of VIII Air Support Command, Brig. Gen. Robert Candee, formulated a plan for a tactical air force implemented with a bomber command, a fighter command controlling two air support divisions, a tactical air service area command, an air defense command and an engineer command. General Candee's document apparently was the first to propose the creation of the latter two commands, the functions of which had previously been considered the responsibility of attached units and other subordinate organizations. The Candee proposals were embodied in a plan for the Ninth Air Force, issued by the United States Army Air Forces in the United Kingdom on 15 October 1943, the day of its activation.

This was the general planning background when Lt. (then Maj.) Gen. Lewis H. Brereton arrived in Britain with his headquarters staff to command the reconstituted Ninth Air Force. Absorbing all elements of the VIII Air Support Command and the VIII Tactical Air Service Area Command the Ninth Air Force was organized with an air service command, a fighter command, a bomber command and a troop carrier command. The original components included a medium and a light bombardment wing, four medium bombardment groups, a reconnaissance group, six air depot groups and the important weather and mobile communications squadrons, which later would send detachments throughout the air force.

The immediate mission of each of the four commands was understood at the outset. Guided by the preliminary planning IX Fighter Command was to assemble fighter and reconnaissance units and to develop tactical air commands (then called air support divisions) to cooperate with the field armies. IX Bomber Command, which as VIII Air Support Command had been operational since late spring 1943, was to furnish the tactical bombing power required by the air force to cooperate with the army group and was to constitute the centralized medium of control for all such bombardment forces. IX Troop Carrier Command was to build to full strength of 14 troop-carrier groups, trained for the most part in the theater according to AAF directives, to deliver airborne infantry and paratroops behind the enemy lines as the opening blow in Europe and to maintain resupply and medical evacuation operations. IX Air Force Service Command was to supply and maintain the tactical units then in existence and to build to sufficient strength to discharge the same service for all the units which would constitute the air force on D-day.

Structurally the new air force headquarters retained the conventional system of organization, with A-1, A-2, A-3, A-4, and the usual special staff sections. In addition, to meet the pressing requirements which swift organizational growth and future operations with the ground forces would entail, deputy chiefs of staff for plans and ground forces liaison were designated.

It was immediately recognized that extensive and rapid planning was required to shape the organization of an air force which would be called upon to perform a relatively new assignment on a scale beyond anything which had yet occurred in tactical air warfare. The

Ninth Air Force was fortunate in that, along with General Brereton, it had a nucleus of higher staff officers who had had considerable experience with the desert tactical campaign in cooperation with the RAF Desert Air Force. The new deputy chief of staff for plans immediately made it plain that the most competent and experienced personnel in all staff sections would be needed to participate in the vast joint planning program initiated by the air force and by higher levels of command in the theater.

On 17 December the Ninth Air Force planning group joined 21st Army group, Allied Expeditionary Air Force, and RAF 2nd Tactical Air Force in the preparation of the air section of the initial joint plan for Operation OVERLORD. The planning at this stage dealt primarily with high-level operational and administrative problems. Meanwhile the new liaison section instituted parallel plans and training programs with the 1st U. S. Army Group and maintained liaison with the RAF on matters of supply, airfields and communications, which were enormously important to an air force newly established in Britain.

One of the major tasks performed by the planning group was the preparation of a troop list (known as the "build-up list") showing by days and beaches the proposed phasing of Ninth Air Force units to the far shore. Other aspects of the planning included diagramming the communications channels between the near and far shore and between fighters in the air and control boats on the sea; logistical data such as tonnage requirements; the airfield construction program; build-up rates; levels of supply and maintenance; the phasing in of operations and movements; and detailed plans of every staff section. The work culminated in the massive Ninth Air Force plan for Operation NEPTUNE, a plan for overwater movement into battle on the continent of the largest air force that ever operated as a unit.

Simultaneously with the broad planning of its participation in Operation OVERLORD the Ninth Air Force set about meeting the many administrative problems involved in constructing this tremendous air force in an extremely short time. Certain deficiencies in the basic planning became immediately apparent, while others appeared later as the magnitude and diversity of tactical responsibilities increased. For the sake of clarity the most important of these deficiencies may be considered without regard to their chronological appearance. The principal deficiencies in the planning proved to be:

a. The misconception in the designation of and requirement for "air support divisions," which was later corrected in their redesignation as, and reorganization into, tactical air commands.

b. The failure to provide initially for War Department authorization to create air defense and engineer commands, which resulted in a long delay in their activation and consequently was detrimental to their operations.

c. The lack of provision in the troop basis for (1) an adequate number of air headquarters to cooperate with the ground armies; i. e., tactical air commands; (2) a central control agency and the necessary administrative units to complete necessary combat crew and replacement training; (3) instrument bombing units; (4) weather reconnaissance units. (These deficiencies were overcome in an undesirable manner by improvising and manipulating tables of organization and equipment; however, there was no practicable alternative to this solution).

d. The seriously inadequate provision for night striking forces and for all types of tactical and technical reconnaissance units.

e. The inadequacy of the truck and motor transport and Ordnance maintenance units assigned to the air force and of the air transport facilities directly controlled by the air force and its commands.

In spite of these and other obstacles, which have been indicated in the previous chapter, the Ninth Air Force gained steadily and rapidly throughout the pre-invasion period as casual personnel and units were received from the Eighth Air Force, the Zone of the Interior and directly from USAAFUK and its successor, USSTAF. Early in December the air force was up to only a quarter of its final tactical strength of 45 operational groups; in February it was half complete; by June—with more than 200,000 officers and men, more than 1,500 tactical, administrative, technical, and service units, and 7 commands—the Ninth had become the largest tactical air force in the history of aerial warfare.

In a study of this scope there is no place for a detailed account of the way in which the Ninth Air Force absorbed, activated, organized, or equipped units, but a discussion of several of the most important trends and influences is appropriate. Generally speaking, tactical organizations arrived in the theater and were absorbed into the air force as complete units, whereas service organizations in large measure were constructed by the air force from technical and administrative personnel shipped from the Zone of the Interior as casuals. The fact that the Ninth was compelled to construct service units in an extremely short time—from personnel who frequently did not have the proper military occupational specialities or training—indicated a lack of constructive planning and appreciation of tactical air requirements which might easily have prejudiced the successful prosecution of the tactical air war.

A related difficulty was that even after the reconstitution of the Ninth Air Force the War Department continued to consider the air forces in Britain as a unit without fully recognizing the distinction between tactical and strategic requirements. For instance, throughout the pre-invasion period fighter aircraft were sent to USAAFUK and later to USSTAF and were not specifically allocated either to the Eighth or Ninth Air Forces. The USSTAF policy of putting first priority on maintaining existing units at full fighter strength worked to the disadvantage of the Ninth Air Force, most of whose tactical groups were new, while most of those in the Eighth were established. Furthermore, when the War Department issued a troop basis on 8 November 1944, no distinction was made between units to be assigned to the Eighth and Ninth and inadequate consideration was given to the special needs of a tactical air component.

The final major influence on the pre-invasion development of the air force was the need for an extensive training program in all units. The entire air force had to be trained for mobility in overland and oversea travel under the most severe combat conditions. In addition, the inadequate preparation of many personnel for their combat jobs compelled the air force to establish extensive and relatively basic training programs within several of the commands, particularly the IX Air Force Service Command. It must be remembered that this training was conducted at the same time that units were preparing for a cross-channel movement, packing, and crating the material to sustain them on the beaches and carrying out an active and increasingly intense air campaign in preparation for the invasion.

The preparation of the individual commands for continental operations was generally and sometimes minutely supervised by Ninth Air Force during the pre-invasion period—particularly in the case of the more unconventional commands.

The plan to create a separate, reasonably autonomous tactical air command to cooperate with each American army in the field meant that the fighter command was responsible for the construction of TACs which would eventually supersede it completely. The fighter command's primary functions were to secure personnel, aircraft and equipment; to set up and develop operational methods and procedures; to train combat personnel; to develop mobility and flexibility in headquarters and tactical units; and to establish liaison with higher and subordinate headquarters which the tactical air commands could inherit when they became fully operational. At the turn of the year IX and XIX Air Support Commands were activated and began a four-month period of growth, organization and reorganization during which their functions were clarified and their designation changed to tactical air commands. Since it was scheduled for prior commitment in the invasion, the IX TAC at first received the bulk of tactical fighter units allocated to the Ninth Air Force and occupied a more important place in the system of operational control of fighter aircraft. In the pre-invasion period fighter command first virtually went out of existence with the construction of the air support commands, then was revived temporarily to function as an operational headquarters for Ninth Air Force fighters in conjunction with RAF 11 Group—particularly the fighters engaged in Operation NEPTUNE.

The development of IX Bomber Command was less complicated than that of the tactical air commands, although it will be seen later that the system of operational control of medium and light bombardment went through a rather involved evolution before it became completely satisfactory. Before the invasion the principal organizational innovation in IX Bomber Command was the provisional activation of a pathfinder squadron which used Oboe equipment for instrument bombing and which later was expanded to the approximate strength of two squadrons. This extremely useful unit was directly under the control of IX Bomber Command headquarters and was administratively equivalent to a group. Later an additional step toward effective all-weather bombing was taken, with the provisional activation of a weather reconnaissance squadron of P–51s directly under command headquarters.

IX Troop Carrier Command's primary problems before D-day were to build from very small beginnings to a strength of more than 1,000 aircraft and more than 2,500 gliders with adequate crews and to maintain an elaborate, secret training program for the opening blow of the invasion. The physical expansion was largely accomplished by the end of March 1944. The tactics and techniques of paradrop, glider tow, parapack in resupply, air landing of supplies, and medical evacuation were mastered in 38 wing and 3 command exercises culminating in the full-scale Exercise EAGLE on 12 May 1944.

The War Department was slow to authorize the hitherto unprecedented engineer and air defense commands, which consequently functioned on an extremely provisional basis throughout the winter of 1943–44. All engineer and air defense units intended for the Ninth Air Force at this time were assigned or attached to air force headquarters and it was not until 30 March, when the War Department approved provisional activation of the engineer and air defense headquarters and headquarters squadrons, that these units were able to function directly under their proper commands. The functions which both commands were to fulfill had a clear place in the general air force commitment. Engineer command was responsible for providing the Ninth Air Force with airfields on the continent, both in the forward areas for fighter-bombers and further back for medium and light bombers. Air defense command's mission was to oppose hostile air action in all areas on the continent occupied by the American forces and behind the Army Group Rear Air Boundary (AGRAB). Originally it was intended that, in addition to signal air warning service and antiaircraft artillery, the air defense command would operate interceptor day and night fighter aircraft. The air force, however, developed a procedure by which day fighters of the TACs could be promptly transferred to air defense operations in the rear when necessary. This necessity, however, did not arise and air defense command never received day fighters. In the autumn of 1944, as the offensive power of the night fighter became needed for night-intruder work and the need for purely defensive night operations appeared negligible, the night fighter squadrons were withdrawn from air defense command and assigned to the TACs.

It has already been explained the IX Air Force Service Command reached full strength primarily through use of casual personnel in activating units in the United Kingdom. The command trained, equipped, and organized hundreds of units before it reached full strength of approximately 60,000 personnel, in 422 units, a week before D-day. The general mission of the service command was to supply and maintain the tactical commands of the Ninth Air Force—with the exception of IX Air Defense Command, which was supplied and maintained by Communications Zone, and IX Engineer Command, which received Class IV engineer supplies from the theater engineer. To perform this mission service command headquarters was organized on the premise that the command would function as A-4 of the air force; instead of the conventional staff system, service command centralized control of almost all subordinate units under 4 major operating divisions—personnel and training; transportation; maintenance; and supply. The second section of this chapter demonstrates how many new functions arose for the command and how these were absorbed by an elastic and flexible application of the existing organization.

At the same time that it was engaged in the complex task of preparing its subordinate units for combat, Ninth Air Force headquarters began the pioneering job of shaping its own internal organization for the almost unprecedented operations which were to follow. One of the most significant lessons learned from tactical air warfare in the desert was that it was mandatory that air and ground cooperating headquarters function together in closest operational and physical unity. The practical step indicated by this thinking was that Ninth Air Force would have to form a mobile, compact operational headquarters which could keep pace with the swiftest movement of the army group and could operate independently of the main administrative headquarters in the rear.

In February 1944 Ninth Air Force operational personnel—who at that time worked closely with their opposite numbers in the 2nd TAF—were organized into an advanced headquarters detachment, which was soon given the authority to issue such general and special orders as were not specifically prohibited by directives of higher headquarters. With this recognition of its official status as a headquarters the advanced detachment grew until it included the Deputy Chief of Staff, Operations; the combat operations section of A-3; the flak reporting, target photo intelligence and research sections of A-2; a large signal detachment; a deputy of the CG, IX Engineer Command; RAF liaison personnel; the headquarters commandant; and individual representatives or small detachments from other staff sections. The newly created tactical research section, organized under A-3 to conduct tactical tests and experiments, was also located at Advanced Headquarters.

The formation of this advanced detachment—which, except for the first 2 months of the invasion, exercised operational control of all tactical units—was the Ninth Air Force's first fundamental departure from standard headquarters organization. In the period before the invasion the establishment of Advanced Headquarters served two purposes: (1) to gain experience before the permanent division of headquarters and (2) to make operational headquarters compact enough to operate adjacent to 2nd TAF.

At the same time IX Fighter Command contributed strongly to the development of mobility in subordinate commands by organizing a "mobile operations" team, the focal point of the command's operations section and the first version of the TAC advanced headquarters. Fighter command instructed its wings and groups to prepare for mobile operations and to eliminate all equipment not absolutely necessary for strictly combat functioning. The command's intimate liaison system with First Army during command post exercises and its "red line" operational communications line were both inherited by IX TAC.

Immediately after the invasion the Ninth Air Force drew an extremely streamlined advanced command post from Advanced Headquarters and established it on the beachhead. This CP was adequately staffed to assume direction of Ninth Air Force operations from Normandy the moment the tactical situation required. The continuation of joint operational planning with 2nd TAF under the broad direction of AEAF, however, meant that under any but the most extraordinary circumstances Advanced Headquarters in England would continue temporarily to maintain operational control. During the first two months of the invasion the Chief of Staff was responsible to the Commanding General for the functioning of Main Headquarters; the Deputy Chief of Staff, Operations, for Advanced Headquarters in the United Kingdom; and the Deputy Commanding General, who had been appointed in late winter to assist the commander, for the advanced command post. (As will be seen, IX Tactical Air Command was cooperating with First Army, the only U. S. army in Normandy during this period, and assumed control of all fighter-bomber and reconnaissance groups as they crossed the channel).

The character of the advanced command post as a compact operational headquartes was simultaneously fortified and weakened during June and July. On the one hand, it was physically adjacent to the headquarters of 12th Army Group after the activation of the latter on 1 August and the army group's G–2 Air and G–3 Air were physically located at the command post, thereby giving a true air-ground team relationship at air force-army group level. On the other hand, as the only Ninth Air Force headquarters component on the continent, the CP attracted a rapidly growing number of administrative responsibilities as various components of administrative sections arrived and claimed that their presence was necessary to coordinate operations in France. When the command post was absorbed by advanced headquarters on 5 August it was considerably oversized and the new forward headquarters was by no means compact enough to move rapidly and frequently. Actually it was essential, however, that many of the administrative sections continue to function partly on the continent.

To resolve this dilemma the Commanding General ordered the early movement of Main Headquarters to France and the elimination of all static or administrative sections and personnel from Advanced as soon as Main arrived on the continent. Meanwhile Advanced Headquarters assumed direct supervisory control of all operations—both by the medium and light bombers in England and the fighter-bombers and reconnaissance planes on the continent. By this time Third Army and XIX Tactical Air Command had become operational on the continent and had established a partnership similar to that of the air force and army group and the IX TAC and First Army. IX ADC had also become operational and, working closely with Communications Zone Headquarters, had established a coordinated air defense of the beaches, ports, air installations, and lines of communication with night fighters, AAA and air warning service.

In September Main Headquarters moved to Chantilly, near Paris, where it remained until the end of the war, establishing and maintaining excellent communications with the administrative headquarters of subordinate commands and almost all the lateral and higher headquarters with which Ninth Air Force was connected in administrative matters—Communications Zone and ETOUSA in Paris, USSTAF Advanced at St. Germain and SHAEF at Versailles. This move established the machinery necessary to execute the Commanding General's order to reduce Advanced Headquarters to only those sections concerned with daily operations. To assure the greatest possible clarity in the distinction between operational and administrative functions and personnel the Ninth Air Force adopted the directorate system of organization in October and for the duration of the war in Europe it did not again employ conventional staff structure.

The new system set up channels of command for operational and administrative staff sections. Two deputy commanding generals, one for operations and one for administration, were designated as responsible for the forward and the rear headquarters respectively. The Deputy Commanding General for Operations, Brig. Gen. Robert M. Lee, had previously been responsible for Advanced Headquarters as Deputy Chief of Staff, Operations. The Deputy Commanding General for Administration, Brig. Gen. Victor H. Strahm, had previously been responsible for Main Headquarters as Chief of Staff and later as Deputy Commanding General in the United Kingdom. Under the directorate system a new chief of staff, normally located at Advanced Headquarters, was responsible for coordination of all functions between the headquarters. Advanced Headquarters included only those directorates which participated in intimate operational liaison with 12th Army Group or in on-the-spot operational control. Other directorates, if required, would be represented at Advanced by individual liaison officers or by small detachments.

As far as the staff sections were concerned, the major change involved in the adoption of the directorate system was the division of A–3 into two separate directorates: the Directorate of Operations, (Advanced Headquarters), charged solely with the conduct of operations, and the Directorate of Plans and Organization, (Main Headquarters), charged with plans, organization, movement, and training. Equal staff status with Operations, Intelligence, Personnel, Supply, and Plans was given to Communications, Reconnaissance, Weather, and Research.

The directorate system proved functionally efficient when Advanced Headquarters was required to operate under canvas with minimum equipment and to make frequent moves. Advanced Headquarters was in essence an operations and intelligence staff close to and in excellent communications with the tactical commands and lateral ground headquarters. For all administration beyond that required in maintaining a command post Advanced was dependent upon Main. The sections at Advanced, equipped to operate in tents and vans with the minimum personnel strength consistent with effectiveness, all had rear echelons to perform the more static phases of their duties at Main Headquarters. The single exception was combat operations, which was assigned entirely to Advanced. As a result of this careful elimination of all personnel, superfluous from the standpoint of operations, Ninth Air Force Advanced Headquarters was smaller than the Advanced Headquarters of either the 9th Bombardment Division or the tactical air commands.

Although the reorganization of Headquarters Ninth Air Force under the directorate system was not a perfect solution to all the organizational problems created by a swiftly changing tactical situation, it is felt that the advantages gained by the adoption of this system substantially outweighed the disadvantages. Perhaps the main disadvantage was that the system was by no means completely satisfactory from the standpoint of the subordinate headquarters. A number of their staff officers did not fully understand the significance of the changes or have the proper conception of the division of responsibility. As a result some administrative confusion arose, particularly with respect to channels of command and communication. In the operational sphere the misunderstanding and confusion which resulted from the adoption of the new system was negligible.

The headquarters organization of the Ninth Air Force remained relatively constant after the adoption of the new structure. Excellent communications were maintained from Advanced Headquarters to lateral ground and air headquarters, to Main Headquarters and to the operational headquarters of the subordinate commands, while Main Headquarters in its strategic location was able to work closely with every major administrative and supply agency in the theater. The highest level coordination between Main and Advanced was performed by the Commanding General, his two deputies and the Chief of Staff, while internal liaison was maintained as part of the operating procedure of each section. In this way Advanced was required to perform only such administrative functions as were necessary to maintain a command post.

A fundamental consideration in the establishment of dual headquarters, which has been referred to only indirectly so far, was the desirability of a division between the operational and administrative components from a communications standpoint. The division of headquarters permitted the economical use of the relatively small number of wire circuits available. Advanced Headquarters was located near the tactical commands, making possible the rapid provision and maintenance of direct and "hot" circuits. Since communications facilities were so important a factor in sustaining the efficient conduct of operations, the signal officer of the Ninth Air Force was always consulted in advance of a proposed relocation of Advanced Headquarters to make sure that the new site was suitable from a communications standpoint. No moves were made until adequate minimum communications had been established at the new headquarters location.

A serious threat to the effective functioning of headquarters appeared in the autumn, when a directive was received from superior headquarters to reorganize Ninth Air Force Headquarters to conform with T/O & E 1–800–18. It was felt that the execution of this directive would have interfered with the conduct of operations. Fortunately, the directive was countermanded when the Commanding General of the Ninth Air Force requested that reorganization be postponed until the end of the war.

As the horizontal (headquarters) organization of air force headquarters was shaped into its final form in the autumn of 1944, the vertical (chain of command) organization of the air force was modified, enlarged in certain directions and contracted in others. In internal problems the Commanding General of the air force kept well-informed about the requirements, difficulties, and opinions of the commands by holding occasional commanders' meetings, at which the air force commander discussed general policy and supervision with his subordinate commanders. These meetings furnished a convenient time and place for consultation with the commanders concerned on any decisions made at air force level affecting the subordinate commands.

In the early autumn of 1944 the Supreme Commander decided that IX Troop Carrier Command should be withdrawn from the Ninth Air Force to form the nucleus of the First Allied Airborne Army. This decision was prompted by the fact that paratroop and airborne elements had grown to approximately the strength of an army and that this enormous and potentially decisive force could best be controlled by Supreme Headquarters through a direct channel of command.

In the field of tactical cooperation the air force commitment became greater as 12th Army Group sent the Ninth Army into the line. This necessitated the formation by the Ninth Air Force of a third tactical air command, the XXIX TAC, formed from elements of the other TACs, the fighter command, the service command and other sources to cooperate with the Ninth Army. The new TAC never had more than provisional status because preliminary plans had not foreseen or investigated the possibilities of the introduction of a third army into 12th Army Group. However, the hurriedly improvised XXIX TAC proved itself just as effective as the two older commands. Since it was Ninth Air Force policy to give subordinate commanders the greatest possible latitude in the organization of their commands, the Commanding General of the XXIX TAC decided to organize his command under the directorate system and continued this system throughout combat. This was the only command in the Ninth Air Force which employed the directorate system during its entire existence in the ETO.

In the autumn of 1944 the Ninth Air Force was required for about 6 weeks to maintain operational and administrative control over XII TAC, which had come up from Italy with the 6th Army Group to invade southern France. This TAC was intended to operate under First Tactical Air Force (Prov), which at this time was still in process of headquarters organization and unable to assume any kind of control. The introduction of the new tactical air force had larger implications, however, than the temporary assumption of control of XII TAC by Ninth Air Force. The preliminary plans, which were intended for all U. S. tactical air power in western Europe, were made on the basis that only one U. S. army group and two armies would be operational on the continent, instead of the two army groups and four armies which were in action from the autumn of 1944 until the end of the war. Thus two air forces and four tactical air commands had to be constructed largely from the personnel and equipment originally intended for one air force and two tactical air commands. This difficult and undesirable situation produced many of the more knotty administrative problems which confronted the Ninth Air Force.

Increasingly apparent, during the progress of operations, became the fact that the wing headquarters were more and more useless appendages except as a source of personnel and equipment to supplement the severely inadequate TAC headquarters T/O & E. When the aircraft control element was integrated with the TAC headquarters the wing headquarters stagnated and became little more than a switching center to the commands' units. It was finally determined that if the TAC had no more than six groups there was no need for a wing headquarters.

An interesting example of the flexibility of command in the European theater occurred during the Ardennes break-through, when 12th Army Group relinquished operational control of the First and Ninth Armies to 21st Army Group and Ninth Air Force transferred operational control of the IX and XXIX TACs to 2nd Tactical Air Force (RAF). First Army and IX TAC returned to their parent organizations in January, but Ninth Army and XXIX TAC continued to be controlled operationally by the British ground and air headquarters until 4 April 1945, when 12th Army Group and Ninth Air Force, respectively, reassumed operational control over their components.

At this point it is appropriate to discuss the administrative aspects of Ninth Air Force operational control. Although this supervisory control in the case of the TACs was designed to give the greatest possible autonomy to the commands in their daily operations, it was never permitted to become superficial or impractically remote. Air force headquarters planned and coordinated all operations conceived at air force-army group or theater level, assigned escort missions and diverted groups from one TAC to another in line with requirements which were normally known only at high level. The extent of this flexibility of group assignment may be seen in the fact that when First Army was the only U. S. army in the field IX TAC controlled 18 fighter-bomber groups; that when XIX TAC became operational on the continent it received 9 of these groups; that when XXIX TAC was activated it was immediately assigned 4 groups—2 from each of the existing TACs—which were cut down to 2 and raised to 5 as Ninth Army operations decreased and increased in relative importance; that, during the battle of the Ardennes, XIX TAC controlled 8 groups and later, as all 3 armies advanced into Germany, the number of groups for each TAC was again equalized; and that, during the last weeks of the war, when only Third Army was active, each of the 2 relatively idle TACs relinquished a group to XIX TAC.

The Ninth Air Force medium and light bombardment force passed through several distinct periods of operational control. At first, when the bombers were used primarily for diversionary attacks on German airfields resisting the passage of Eighth Air Force heavy bombers, through USAAFUK and later USSTAF, designated target priorities for Ninth Air Force operations. This practice was to a certain extent incompatible with the proper development of the tactical air force, since it meant that ultimate control of its bombardment power was vested in a command which had completely different objectives in view. Within Eighth Air Force requirements Ninth Air Force issued general directives establishing priorities for targets by types and IX Bomber Command selected targets from these directives and planned missions against them. This procedure remained in effect only until air force combat operations had perfected its organization to the point where it could assume more detailed control of operations.

Early in March 1944, Headquarters, Allied Expeditionary Air Forces (AEAF), assumed operational control of Ninth Air Force and the 2nd TAF (RAF), releasing the tactical air force from USSTAF operational control. AEAF generally prescribed the percentage of effort to be expended on each type of target on a long-term basis and Ninth Air Force Advanced Headquarters began to select targets and plan missions for IX Bomber Command. The reasons for this assumption of detailed operational control of IX Bomber Command were: (1) that mission planning could best be performed at the level which controlled, and therefore could coordinate, the operations of bombers and fighter-bombers; (2) that air force maintained intimate operational liaison with the ground forces while the bomber command did not; and (3) that air force worked with the 2nd TAF in planning the total, coordinated tactical air campaign.

The ultimate procedure which was put into effect when Advanced Headquarters became operational on the continent was for the Ninth Air Force to select targets, to specify the time and weight of attacks and to provide necessary fighter escort from the TACs while bomber command arranged all further details. The only general departure from this system was during the transfer of the first bomber groups to France, when air force controlled all details of bombardment operations until the advanced headquarters of the bomber command was established on the continent.

B. ORGANIZATION OF COMMANDS

1. IX Fighter Command

The IX Fighter Command, as reconstituted in the United Kingdom on 16 October 1943, had the fundamental mission of building, training, and equipping tactical air commands, known first as air support divisions, until they were fully prepared to carry out Phase 1, 2, and 3 tactical air operations in autonomous cooperation with U. S. armies in the field. The fighter command worked toward its own dissolution because, when the tactical air commands began autonomous operations with the armies in France, it became a mere paper organization without operational functions.

The object of IX Fighter Command's training program was to qualify all units for combat operations at the earliest possible time. A minimum of 6 weeks of specialized training was prescribed for all units to "work the kinks out of" their modified organizations and learn how to accomplish their special mission. All aspects of combat training were given highest precedence.

The IX Fighter Command, in the absence of a fully developed air support command, had directed all operations of its tactical units through December 1943 and January 1944. Then the IX ASC (TAC) took over control of operations and training through February, March and part of April 1944. Then, again in the "Uxbridge period," the latter part of April, May, and June, IX Fighter Command was revived as a convenient and practical means of unifying Ninth Air Force fighter operational control in Britain before, during, and after invasion, and especially during the movement of IX TAC Headquarters and the many fighter-bomber and reconnaissance groups to France.

In November 1943 Ninth Air Force issued tables of organization for the IX Fighter Command, the two air support divisions and subordinate tactical units. This was followed by the activation of the IX Air Support Command in December 1943 and of the XIX Air Support Command in January 1944. Although the two air support commands were intended ultimately to be equal in strength, the bulk of tactical units received by the Ninth Air Force were assigned initially to the IX Air Support Command, which would be the first to become operational on the continent.

At the end of January 1944, when it was apparent that the air support commands would replace IX Fighter Command as operational headquarters, General Quesada, redesignated commander of IX Air Support Command, assumed control of all Ninth Air Force fighter and reconnaissance groups and received all fighter command personnel and equipment for the organization, training, and operation of the two air support commands. Tactical units continued to be assigned to the IX ASC (TAC), in line with the policy first to build up this command and later to divert half of the tactical strength to XIX ASC (TAC) when Third Army began operations. At this time Ninth Air Force specified that T/O authorizations for the air support commands would not be exceeded and that filler personnel would be assigned to IX Fighter Command (which continued to exist on paper) for detached service with the ASC (TAC) units.

At a Ninth Air Force commanders' meeting on 27 February 1944, General Quesada received authority to re-activate the IX Fighter Command, on a purely temporary basis, to function as an operational headquarters in conjunction with RAF 11 Group at Uxbridge, England. That this arrangement was only temporary was obvious, because General Quesada retained command of the IX Air Support Command. General Weyland was named deputy commander of IX Fighter Command while retaining command of XIX ASC.

The resumption of operational control by Headquarters, IX Fighter Command, did not imply a decline in the activities of the air support commands, which on 18 April 1944, were redesignated tactical air commands. Operations personnel from both headquarters manned the fighter command operational headquarters at Uxbridge and were also temporarily assigned to wings and groups to gain practical experience. In addition, the administrative sections of the IX TAC performed all necessary functions of that nature for IX Fighter Command.

Under IX Fighter Command the collective strength of the two tactical air commands increased from fewer than 11,000 officers and enlisted men in December 1943 to more than 35,000 in May 1944. The most difficult problem which confronted IX Fighter Command in the pre-invasion period was the acquisition of an adequate number of fighter aircraft for tactical units. This acute problem had vital organizational and procedural consequences in both the A–3 and A–4 staff sections of Headquarters Ninth Air Force and in its commands.

With the landing of American troops in Normandy the IX Tactical Air Command began independent operation in cooperation with the First U. S. Army. The mechanics of transferring groups from the operational control of IX Fighter Command to that of the IX TAC was simple. IX TAC established headquarters in Normandy and assumed control of all fighter groups as soon as they reached the continent.

During the transitional period of movement to the continent General Weyland, commander of the XIX TAC, controlled all fighter-bomber groups remaining at British bases through the IX Fighter Command operational headquarters at Uxbridge. When the last group moved to France IX Fighter Command was operationally dissolved. It remained on inactive status throughout the Battle of Europe and its table of organization was used to bring the tactical air commands to full required operating strength.

2. IX Tactical Air Command

It has been explained that the IX TAC initially received most of the tactical fighter elements allocated to the Ninth Air Force. After D-day, when IX TAC established headquarters in France, it assumed operational control of all fighter-bomber groups as they moved to the continent.

By the end of June 1944 five fighter-bomber groups were conducting full-scale operations on the continent. The working unity of IX TAC and First Army, their physical proximity and the ease and rapidity of operational communications resulted in an increase in the efficiency and the flexibility of the fighter-bomber force.

In this early period first battle tests increased the effectiveness of fighter-bomber operations in cooperation with the ground forces. These procedures involved the increasingly precise control of airborne fighter-bombers by means of reconnaissance aircraft, tactical control centers, and tactical air liaison parties, in line with the minute-by-minute ground developments and air requirements known at TAC combat operations. The functional organization and operating procedures that were developed and tested in the Normandy campaign, with particular reference to combat operations and ground-to-air communications, were basically employed by the other TACs as they became operational.

The division of functions in TAC headquarters, modeled after the separation of operational and administrative functions in Advanced and Main Headquarters by the Ninth Air Force, was the surest manner of maintaining the necessary close connection with the army, no matter how rapidly it advanced. IX TAC, for instance, maintained a dual headquarters during the Normandy and northern France campaigns. It was found thereafter that a single consolidated headquarters could usually be established adjacent to First Army. When First Army's CP moved rapidly IX TAC dispatched with it a small, operational "super-advanced" headquarters, consisting of the Commanding General, an A–3 officer, an A–2 officer, and signal personnel, to assure close cooperation in all joint air-ground operations.

Except for the weeks immediately following D-day IX TAC's operational strength varied from a maximum strength of 9 fighter-bomber groups in August 1944 to 4 in December 1944 and April 1945, in line with decisions by the Commanding General of the Ninth Air Force on the proper disposition of his total fighter-bomber force.

The most important policy regarding the command and control of elements within IX TAC was that of maintaining flexibility. In Normandy IX TAC headquarters retained operational control of all groups but assigned administrative control to 70th Fighter Wing. During the relatively static period after the sweep across France IX TAC Headquarters assumed administrative as well as operational control of its groups. When the Ardennes counter-offensive disrupted communications IX TAC divided its headquarters into Advanced and Rear, leaving operational control with Advanced and delegating administrative control to Rear. After the Ardennes thrust was repulsed IX TAC's Advanced and Rear Headquarters were again consolidated and remained together until the end of hostilities.

3. XIX Tactical Air Command

The XIX Tactical Air Command became operational, in cooperation with the Third Army, on the continent on 1 August 1944. Its elements consisted of some of the fighter-bomber groups already tested in battle under the IX Tactical Air Command. This new XIX TAC-Third Army team swept through the breach at St. Lo which the First

Army had opened in the German lines, cleared the Brittany Peninsula, closed one jaw of the Argentan-Falaise gap and swept across France to the Siegfried Line in the most spectacular demonstration of air-ground cooperation the world had ever seen.

XIX TAC divided its headquarters into Advanced and Rear during the entire period of its operations on the continent. Combat operations were planned and directed by the Commanding General from Advanced Headquarters, which consisted chiefly of operations, intelligence, and signal personnel and a small detachment of the necessary administrative personnel. Administrative functions were centered at Rear Headquarters, which was normally located in the vicinity of the tactical units and was moved far less frequently than Advanced Headquarters. Under certain conditions Rear Headquarters assumed the operational function of a wing, relaying orders to the groups and consolidating and forwarding reports from the groups.

During periods of most rapid movement Advanced Headquarters normally moved to a new location about 2 days after Third Army moved its CP. This interim period was covered by an "X-ray" echelon of the Advanced Headquarters, consisting of the chief of staff and two or three assistants, which moved with Third Army and stayed with it until the Advanced Headquarters moved up. Their function was to maintain personal liaison at all times.

In the sweep across France units were so widely scattered throughout the area from Brest to Belgium, a distance of more than 500 miles, that it became necessary at one time to divide the headquarters into four components, one to administer and coordinate operations of groups in the beach-head area, a rear headquarters to perform administration, an advanced headquarters to coordinate the operational activity of groups other than those located on the beach-head, and the X-ray detachment that moved with the highly mobile Third Army Headquarters. The X-ray echelon did not assume control of operations, but it insured uninterrupted liaison at all times.

4. XXIX Tactical Air Command (Prov)

The XXIX Tactical Air Command (Prov), only major command of the Ninth Air Force organized after D-day, was activated late in September 1944, when the Ninth Army moved up to the western front, in line with the policy of establishing a separate autonomous tactical air command to cooperate with each army. The TAC became operational in early October 1944, a little more than 2 weeks after the initial orders for its organization had been issued.

This command headquarters was formed by the assignment of two fighter wing headquarters and filling in the cracks in the tactical air command picture with numerous small detachments. These detachments were furnished by the IX Tactical Air Command, the XIX Tactical Air Command, the IX Air Force Service Command, the IX Air Defense Command, and from the bulk allotment of troops available to Ninth Air Force Headquarters. The XXIX Tactical Air Command Headquarters was organized, throughout its history, under the directorate system of control, with deputy commanders for operations and administration. The Commanding General, Ninth Air Force, selected Brig. Gen. Richard E. Nugent, formerly Deputy Commanding General for Operations, Ninth Air Force, as the XXIX Tactical Air Command commander. The headquarters functioned as one installation, except in emergency or when the headquarters advanced. When the headquarters advanced the advanced or operational element moved forward and was followed as soon as communications permitted by the rear or administrative complement. Similarly, during the Ardennes counter-offensive emergency, when the headquarters was in danger of being overrun, the administrative elements were moved farther to the rear, with duplicate operations equipment, so that if the operational headquarters were overrun the command could function immediately from the rear headquarters. The advanced operational headquarters was at all times in the immediate vicinity of Ninth Army Headquarters.

During the entire operational period the XXIX Tactical Air Command moved its command headquarters in leap-frog fashion, with duplicate operational equipment. One set of equipment would be moved forward early and set up in operation in an advanced position. When communications had been established with the Ninth Army Headquarters, Ninth Air Force Headquarters, advanced Ninth Army elements and subordinate XXIX Tactical Air Command units, control would pass from the rear operating equipment to the forward operating equipment. The administrative and supply difficulties in securing proper equipment and administration, not only for a provisional tactical air command but also for provisional units within the provisional tactical air command, were enormous. It was only through excellent support from Ninth Army Headquarters, including a complete disregard of many supply and financial army regulations, that this command could function.

This youngest tactical air command was formed with the minimum essentials to meet its responsibilities and thus was more compact and more streamlined than the other TACs. Its staff members as well as its combat groups were, however, experienced in combat at the time of the tactical air command's formation and quickly and effectively began to cooperate with the Ninth Army.

5. XII Tactical Air Command

The XII Tactical Air Command, prior to the invasion of southern France, was a component of the Twelfth Air Force. The XII TAC had provided a large share of all air cooperation for Seventh Army on the way up through southern France and, when Third and Seventh Armies linked to form a solid front, late in September 1944, it came under the temporary control of the Ninth Air Force.

For about 6 weeks, while the First Tactical Air Force (Prov) was being organized, the Ninth Air Force assumed both administrative and operational control of XII TAC and all assigned units. Thus for a time the Ninth was responsible for the operations of four tactical air commands. First Tactical Air Force (Prov) was established 25 October 1944, but it had not yet been organized. Ninth Air Force, by verbal agreement, continued to administer, supply and control all XII TAC units until mid-November, when First TAF assumed full responsibility and control.

The Ninth Air Force transferred three fighter-bomber groups with their ancillary units, as well as an air depot group, service groups and weather units, to the XII TAC. This transfer of tactical and ancillary units gave the needed strength to the XII TAC to assume proper coordination and cooperation with the U. S. Seventh Army.

6. 9th Bombardment Division

On 16 October 1943, Maj. Gen. (then Col.) Samuel E. Anderson was named commander of IX Bomber Command, which had been activated in the Middle East and was then in transit to the European Theater of Operations. The development of the IX Bomber Command was an outgrowth of the Bradley Plan, but included numerous modifications. IX Bomber Command, as it was eventually constituted, included eight medium bomber groups and three light bomber groups.

Headquarters and Headquarters Squadron, 3rd Bombardment Wing (M), and four medium bombardment groups under the wing, were the basic units assigned to IX Bomber Command (M) on 16 October 1943. All these units had been operational under VIII Air Support Command and had been reassigned to Ninth Air Force the previous day by Headquarters, USAAF, United Kingdom.

In November 1943, with the completion of the movement of Headquarters and Headquarters Squadron, IX Bomber Command, from the Middle East, 3rd Bombardment Wing (M) was redesignated 98th Combat Bombardment Wing (M). The nucleus from Africa was augmented by personnel drawn from the 98th Wing to complete the organization of the reconstituted Headquarters and Headquarters Squadron, IX Bomber Command. The majority of the headquarters personnel came from the 98th Wing, which continued, however, to exist as an operational unit under IX Bomber Command.

IX Bomber Command was brought to its full operational strength during the next 6 months by the assignment of tactical units brought from the Zone of the Interior and ancillary units for the most part activated in the theater and staffed by casual personnel. In the period from January to August 1944, the command's personnel strength increased from more than 13,000 to approximately 23,000 officers and enlisted men. Growth was most rapid in March and April 1944.

The build-up of IX Bomber Command to its full strength took place between 16 October 1943 and 4 April 1944, particularly in February and March. On 12 November 1943, a series of Ninth Air Force orders established the 97th, 98th, and 99th Combat Bombardment Wings. The 97th Combat Bombardment Wing (L) was a completely new combat organization. The medium bombardment groups were divided evenly betwen the 98th and 99th Wings and the three light bombardment groups were placed under the control of the 97th Wing.

Certain major organizational changes in IX Bomber Command were produced under the stimulus of combat. The use of Oboe equipment for instrument bombing led to the organization of the First Pathfinder Squadron (Prov) in February 1944. A provisional weather reconnaissance squadron was also activated. Both units were placed directly under the control of IX Bomber Command Headquarters. These two provisional organizations were essential and successful, but presented administrative difficulties in the absence of proper tables of organization, which necessitated using personnel from within the command and for which no provisions had been made under War Department authorization.

IX Bomber Command, later redesignated 9th Bombardment Division, was unique among Ninth Air Force tactical units in that it was operational at the time it came under the jurisdiction of the reconstituted Ninth Air Force. The Eighth Air Force had been employing the medium bombers of the VIII Air Support Command to support its strategic heavy bomber missions by assigning attacks on enemy fighter airfields along the French, Belgium, and Dutch coasts to the command. For a comparatively long period after IX Bomber Command assumed control of the medium bomber groups Eighth Air Force continued to exercise priority, coordinating through USAAFUK and its successor USSTAF, on all U. S. air effort from the United Kingdom. (See previous section, this chapter, for an account of the evolution of IX Bomber Command operational control.)

The 9th Bombardment Division maintained a single headquarters throughout the entire operational period except during the transfer of its tactical units to the continent. Advanced Headquarters, Ninth Air Force, during this period, assumed immediate direction of bombardment wings and groups until tactical Advanced Headquarters, IX Bomber Command, was established on the far shore. When all bombardment units had been moved to the continent, IX Bomber Command again consolidated its headquarters.

7. IX Troop Carrier Command

IX Troop Carrier Command, activated on 16 October 1943, initially consisted of a cadre of six officers from Headquarters, First Troop Carrier Command, still in the ZI.

A troop carrier wing and three troop carrier groups were assigned to the command in October and November 1943. Evolution of the command was accelerated in February 1944 by the assignment of a second troop carrier wing and two additional troop carrier groups. March witnessed expansion on a sufficiently large scale to build up the command to full organizational strength by the assignment of a third wing and nine more groups.

The build-up of IX Troop Carrier Command was accomplished, for the most part, between December 1943 and March 1944. Command personnel at the end of January 1944 totaled more than 8,500. By the end of March 1944, 65 of the 161 units which were to comprise the command had been organized. "Ninth Air Force troop requirements," dated 25 April 1944, showed that 3 troop-carrier wings and 14 troop-carrier groups had been allocated to the IX Troop Carrier Command and all but half of one group were present.

(An indication of the growth in operational strength of the command may be seen in the increase of C–47 and C–53 type aircraft from 353 in February to 1,226 by May 1944. Each troop-carrier group was authorized 64 aircraft and a reserve of 25 percent, totaling 80 aircraft. Two combat crews manned each aircraft.)

That the air force should control airborne training because it had the means was recognized by Headquarters, Army Air Forces, which on 28 December 1943, recommended that necessary command and/or staff agencies be established on the highest air levels to handle airborne training and operations. The tremendous contribution made by IX Troop Carrier Command to the success of the invasion reflected the thorough and arduous training undergone prior to 27 May 1944. Paradrop, the glider tow, the use of the parapack in resupply, air landing of supplies and medical evacuation were practiced in 38 wing and 3 command exercises which culminated in the full-scale invasion rehearsal (Exercise EAGLE) on 12 May 1944.

Early in 1944 all troop carrier command units were ordered to be fully prepared to perform their assigned mission prior to Y-day (1 June) and training in general was immediately divided into the following classes: individual, organizational and operational.

To meet the absolute necessity for expert navigation in airborne operations a pathfinder school was established by Headquarters, IX Troop Carrier Command, on 1 March 1944. Intensive training was given carefully selected pathfinder crews in the use of all aids which enable a navigator to pinpoint his position in normal, night, or instrument weather and in the procedure of dropping on landing and drop zones personnel equipped with radio beacons, flares, and other devices to guide the aircraft and glider trains.

The airborne invasion of Normandy and subsequent supply and evacuation operations were the principal accomplishments of IX Troop Carrier Command during the three operational months it remained assigned to the Ninth Air Force.

On 10 July 1944, orders were issued sending the 50th and 53rd Troop Carrier Wings from the United Kingdom to Italy to be used in the invasion of southern France. Units used in this operation temporarily passed out of control of the IX Troop Carrier Command. Maj. Gen. Paul L. Williams, commanding the two wings, arrived in Italy on 16 July 1944, and activated the provisional troop carrier air division to carry out the invasion mission.

By late summer of 1944 the First Allied Airborne Army was organized to perform all future airborne missions of Allied military forces, both in the delivery of troops to their drop zones and in commanding them before the drop. It followed logically that IX Troop Carrier Command would form a keystone of the new army. On 1 September 1944, IX Troop Carrier Command was assigned to U. S. Strategic Air Forces for administrative control and was attached to the First Allied Airborne Army for operational control.

8. IX Air Defense Command

The IX Air Defense Command figured in preliminary air force planning, but its Headquarters and Headquarters Squadron was not provisionally activated until 30 March 1944. The delay was caused by indecision concerning the proper tables of organization and equipment for the command, which had no precedent in other air forces. The projected organization of IX Air Defense Command was evolved under the direction of Brig. Gen. William L. Richardson, former Eighth Air Force antiaircraft officer, who was appointed Commanding General of the IX Air Defense Command on 29 December 1944.

Another factor that retarded the development of IX Air Defense Command was the fact that, pending approval of the organization by Headquarters, Army Air Forces, personnel were drawn on a purely temporary basis from Ninth Air Force Headquarters and replacement depots.

The actual development of IX Air Defense Command began in January 1944, when one AA artillery brigade and one AA group were assigned to the Ninth Air Force. The personnel of these units were employed temporarily in command headquarters, which was designated Air Defense Headquarters of Ninth Air Force, until the War Department approved the provisional activation of IX Air Defense Command.

Air defense headquarters immediately assumed control of all Ninth Air Force units then engaged in the defense of airdromes in the United Kingdom and functioned, in effect, as a regularly constituted command.

After provisional activation on 30 March 1944, Headquarters and Headquarters Squadron, IX Air Defense Command, was officially activated on 22 May 1944. By this time administrative channels had been established with Headquarters Ninth Air Force. Supplies and equipment peculiar to air defense, as well as all initial T/E equipment, were obtained from Communications Zone depots. Class I supplies and certain Class II supplies were furnished by IX Air Force Service Command.

IX Air Defense Command headquarters was organized along conventional lines, with the Deputy Commander for Operations controlling the A-2, A-3, and Signals sections, and the Deputy Commander for Administration controlling A-1, A-4, and most of the special staff sections. Except for the period of movement to the continent and the advance into Germany, the command did not find it necessary to divide into advanced and main headquarters.

To perform its mission of air defense the command had assigned to it: (1) up to eight AAA brigades, with AAA groups, battalions, and operations detachments attached; (2) the 71st Fighter Wing (which functioned as a part of the command headquarters) and two U. S. night fighter squadrons; (3) two signal air warning battalions and two fighter control squadrons. Attached for operations initially were two sectors of 85 Group, TAF, which included British air warning, fighter control and night fighter units. These units were added because American units available were inadequate for the task.

Operations were under the immediate charge of two provisional air defense wings (U. S.) and the two RAF sectors, each of which was assigned an area of responsibility and given operational control over designated AAA, air warning and night fighter units. Later, when the Luftwaffe was no longer capable of major operations against our rear areas, the RAF units and our own night fighter squadrons were released for other employment, the provisional air defense wings were inactivated and the AAA brigade headquarters became the main subordinate operating echelon.

The command headquarters assigned missions and areas of responsibility, allocated available means and was primarily responsible for all supply, administration, and maintenance.

Original air force planning for the command had contemplated air force command of all AAA except that engaged in close defense of ground force elements at the front, but this was not acceptable to some of the ground and service commanders. As the campaign progressed, however, the Supreme Commander decided that this was essential and directed first the attachment and later outright assignment of all such AAA to the IX ADC. The strength of the command reached a peak of some 43,000 officers and men in the winter of 1944–45 and its area of responsibility extended from the channel into Germany and from Antwerp to Marseille.

The antiaircraft units which had been attached to the Ninth Air Force in February and March 1944 were employed in the defense of air force airdromes until shortly before D-day, when they were released to the ground forces. Two important policies were evolved while the AAA units operated with Ninth Air Force bombardment and fighter-bomber groups: (1) that an AAA brigade with attached units be responsible for the air defense of each tactical air command and of IX Bomber Command; and (2) that such brigades establish their headquarters adjacent to the TAC and bomber command headquarters.

Two signal air warning battalions and two P–61 night fighter squadrons were assigned to IX Air Defense Command in March and April 1944, as its warning and interception elements.

A tactical training area was established in Britain, where the warning, fighter, and antiaircraft components received practical instructions in integrated operations. The training period showed the value of searchlight battalions, which were subsequently adopted wherever possible in the Ninth Air Force. The number of assigned or attached searchlight battalions was never sufficient for full coverage of IX Air Defense Command's area of responsibility.

IX Air Defense Command established advanced headquarters in Normandy on 20 June 1944, and the remainder of the headquarters had crossed the channel to reconsolidate by 28 July. Operational control of the night fighter squadrons from the continent began late in July.

A basic responsibility of IX Air Defense Command had always been the defense of Ninth Air Force fields. The rapid movement of operational bases toward the front, however, raised the question whether antiaircraft units on fields within army areas would be commanded by IX Air Defense Command or by the ground forces. This issue was ultimately decided on 19 January 1945, when SHAEF instructed that an Army Group Rear Air Boundary be established, that the army assume responsibility for the air defense of all installations forward of that boundary and that IX Air Defense Command be responsible for the air defense of all installations rear of the boundary. The boundary was established by the commanding generals of the 12th Army Group and the Ninth Air Force in such a way that all airfields were in the rear area.

9. IX Engineer Command

Early in 1943, when it appeared that the U. S. tactical air force for the invasion would be developed within the Eighth Air Force, plans were made to establish an engineer division in the VIII Air Support Command. After the reconstitution of the Ninth Air Force these plans took definite shape with General Brereton's approval of a proposal to organize an independent engineer command rather than to have engineer functions performed by a staff section at air force headquarters. The fact that operations in the ETO would require 20,000 engineer aviation troops working in all army areas and base sections largely determined this decision.

The first practical step in the formation of IX Engineer Command was the approval by Ninth Air Force, USAAFUK and ETOUSA of a complete T/O & E for command headquarters and a list of subordinate units prepared by the Engineer, Ninth Air Force. The War Department, however, was slow to approve the recommended organization, because there was no precedent for an engineer command and some uncertainty as to whether one was necessary or desirable in the ETO or in any other theater. Nevertheless the Engineer, Ninth Air Force, was authorized in the theater to proceed with the organization of command headquarters as part of Headquarters Ninth Air Force, with the initial training of units and with participation in plans for Operation OVERLORD. After a short period, when the headquarters was organized functionally in four divisions (Administration, Intelligence, Troops and Construction), it adopted conventional staff organization.

On 25 January 1944 Brig. Gen. James B. Newman, Jr., assumed command of Engineer Headquarters, Ninth Air Force, and within a month the still unauthorized headquarters reached almost full strength, completed training of four battalions and acquired an additional regiment of four battalions and certain ancillary units. Although progress continued at a reasonable pace in February and March, the embryo organization worked against difficulties and delays naturally incident to the operation of an unauthorized command functioning under informal recognition. It was obviously difficult to secure necessary supplies and equipment, but the commander of the Ninth Air Force assisted materially by authorizing issue of adequate signal equipment to assure communications between all elements of the proposed command. Future events established the wisdom of this decision, for engineers have been notoriously weak in communications and have generally had to depend upon facilities of the units which they served. IX Engineer Command was thus spared the usual delays in transmission of instructions and receipt of reports. In March 1944 it was estimated that adequate organic communications would increase the output of the command by at least one airfield a week, but later experience showed that this was a conservative estimate and that IX Engineer Command was fortunate in being assigned to an air force which made signal facilities available to it. Another important development, during the period before provisional activation of the command, was the receipt of the first aircraft for its flight section. The assignment of aircraft to the command permitted rapid transportation of supervisory personnel as well as air reconnaissance to supplement ground reconnaissance in the location of prospective airfield sites.

IX Engineer Command was activated provisionally on 30 March 1944, by the Ninth Air Force, after the receipt of a bulk allotment from the War Department which provided most of the required grades and ratings. Progress in all phases of operations was immediately apparent and the few remaining technicalities were eliminated by the formal activation of the command on 1 July 1944. By D-day the command consisted of headquarters and headquarters squadron, an engineer air force headquarters company, 1 camouflage and 3 airborne engineer aviation battalions, 4 aviation regimental headquarters and H & S companies, 16 engineer aviation battalions and 4 combat communications teams, in addition to MP, medical, ordnance, and quartermaster detachments and a third engineer maintenance company en route to the ETO. The command included more than 17,000 officers and enlisted men.

The chain of command at this time was from command through regiment to battalion and from command directly to ancillary unit. The airborne and camouflage battalions operated directly under command headquarters; they were never used for their primary mission, but later functioned in airfield maintenance and operation of Class IV and other supply dumps. The engineer aviation battalions were attached to regimental headquarters so that they could be shifted freely between regiments when necessary.

The headquarters moved to Normandy in five echelons, the first on D-day under the deputy commander and the second on D plus 5, to form an operational component which would control all elements ashore. The administrative component followed in three echelons, the last of which arranged supplies from Britain until D plus 90. The command functioned smoothly on the beachhead in the construction of airfields and maintenance of airfields in the army area (and assistance to IX Air Force Service Command in the maintenance of Communications Zone airfields), as well as supervision of camouflage and water supply, operation of a reproduction service and maintenance of roads to Ninth Air Force installations. This work was executed without basic change in the command's vertical and horizontal organization set up in Britain.

As early as March 1944 plans for the Operation OVERLORD indicated that the dispersion of units after the break-out from the beachhead would increase the difficulty of operational control. To meet this problem it was decided that the command would be divided into two brigades. Commanders of these brigades were to operate abreast, assuming responsibility for operations in areas designated by command headquarters. Administrative channels were to remain unchanged.

In early August 1944 the two brigades were activated to support IX and XIX TACs. Command headquarters continued to control operations, allocate troops and equipment to brigades and dictate general policies from the viewpoint of the Ninth Air Force as a whole; brigades, however, were given the widest possible latitude in meeting the requirements of the TACs. The success of this plan was immediately apparent, with the result that the system was employed for the remainder of the European campaign.

By 17 August airfield maintenance had become a major problem, with fields in the beachhead area as well as under construction in Brittany and all brigade and regimental headquarters engaged in establishing clutches near Le Mans and reconnaissance toward Paris. Accordingly the First Airfield Maintenance Regiment (Provisional) was organized, with the last heavy battalion to arrive and the three airborne battalions, to maintain all the Normandy fields under the Engineer, IX Air Force Service Command. It soon became obvious that this arrangement was unworkable, due to lack of headquarters personnel and communications equipment. On 5 September, when the maintenance problem had moved forward to Le Mans-Orleans-Paris, the IX Air Force Service Command relinquished responsibilities for maintenance of Com Z airfields to IX Engineer Command, which was then charged with maintenance of rear and forward airfields and installations. Later, when USSTAF, XII TAC, and ATC appeared on the continent, the strength of the maintenance forces was increased to avoid overextending the area and construction efforts of the first and second brigades in support of forward elements of the Ninth Air Force. Accordingly a third brigade was activated by attaching units previously employed by the two construction brigades and by adding a regiment and several battalions from the United Kingdom. The peak military strength of this brigade was reached at about the time of its activation. As the extent of civilian participation in rear area work increased, engineer troops were removed from the Third Brigade and attached to the First and Second Brigades. During the last several weeks of operations just prior to VE-day the Third Brigade was charged with maintenance and construction of all fields and installations in the U. S. area west of the Rhine River and, in so doing, employed less than the equivalent of five engineer aviation battalions.

In October 1944 IX Engineer Command Headquarters was divided into a forward operational component and a rear administrative component, parallel to the Ninth Air Force dual headquarters. This split was essential because command headquarters near Paris was losing touch with the brigades in the Nancy and Charleroi areas and with Advanced Headquarters, Ninth Air Force, at Verdun. This final split stretched the command's resources in housekeeping and MP personnel, signal equipment and transportation almost to the breaking point.

Meanwhile several new developments occurred which affected IX Engineer Command operations to some extent. USSTAF Advanced Headquarters, which controlled the 27th Transport Wing, moved to the Paris area; the First Allied Airborne Army required airfields for the Arnhem operation; and the First Tactical Air Force was being formed and needed bases in the Dijon-Nancy-Luxeuil area. To meet these new commitments USSTAF and First TAF engineer commands were formed to assume engineer responsibilities for their parent air forces. The decision to establish two new engineer commands, without adequate personnel, equipment or supply channels, showed the importance attached by each air force commander to control over the engineer troops constructing his airfields. IX Engineer Command assisted the new commands in establishing supply and communications channels, setting up construction standards and adopting operating procedures, but even so the system did not work satisfactorily and on 8 November 1944, all units of the two commands were attached to IX Engineer Command for administration and supply.

Since the First TAF Engineer Command (actually a regimental headquarters with three battalions) could not handle all construction and maintenance for the new air force, IX Engineer Command assigned to its Second Brigade responsibility for new construction for XII TAC in the Nancy area. This arrangement was made by agreement between the commanders of the two air forces.

On 20 February 1945 USSTAF assumed direct command of all aviation engineer troops in the ETO and authorized the activation of Engineer Command, USSTAF, including IX Engineer Command and the provisional engineer commands which had been functioning for USSTAF and the First TAF. The new command was charged with engineer work for all U. S. air elements in Europe.

While this development increased the scope of the work and caused what seemed to be a major organizational change, it actually did not change relations significantly between Ninth Air Force and IX Engineer Command. The command's main headquarters near Paris was strengthened by the addition of a few A–3 personnel and became the new Headquarters Engineer Command (Prov) USSTAF. The former advanced headquarters was redesignated Headquarters IX Engineer Command and the First and Second Brigades, attached to it, were charged with construction and maintenance in forward areas for the IX, XIX and XXIX TACs and the First TAF. The Third Brigade, operating directly under the new USSTAF engineer command headquarters, was responsible for similar duties in the Communications Zone. Units which had served USSTAF or First TAF in the preceding period were attached to IX Engineer Command or Third Brigade as required. Thus the name of the command had been changed, its strength had been increased to more than 23,000 and its sphere of responsibilty had been expanded, but IX Engineer Command continued to function without a noticeable organizational change. All administration was direct from USSTAF Engineer Command headquarters to regiments, while operations were conducted with great latitude by IX Engineer Command and Third Brigade under the broad supervision of USSTAF Engineer Command.

After the end of the war the command was removed from USSTAF and returned to Ninth Air Force control as Headquarters IX Engineer Command (Main) exactly as if no temporary change in name had occurred.

10. IX Air Force Service Command

The organization of IX Air Force Service Command was largely anticipated in the Bradley Plan. On 16 October 1943, IX Air Service Command (redesignated IX Air Force Service Command in January 1944), was reconstituted in the ETO under Maj. Gen. Henry J. F. Miller. The command's first constituents were Headquarters, IX Air Service Command, from the Middle East, and the VIII Tactical Air Service Area Command, with 6 air depot groups. The original strength was multiplied almost 1,000 percent, to a personnel strength of more than 62,600 officers and enlisted men by July 1944.

The mission of the command was to supply and maintain (beyond the limits of first and second echelons) the tactical commands of the Ninth Air Force, with the exception of the air defense command, which was supplied and maintained by the ground forces, and the IX Engineer Command, which received engineer supplies from the theater engineer but all other supplies through service command.

To fulfill its mission the command was charged with the following general functions:

a. The procurement, storage and issue of all items of supply and equipment for all units of the Ninth Air Force.

b. Command, technical control and supervision of all activities of the Ninth Air Force, insofar as they pertained to assembly, maintenance, repair, overhaul, modification, salvage and reclamation of Ninth Air Force supplies and equipment beyond the responsibilities of the first and second echelons of maintenance.

c. Command and technical control of all Ninth Air Force depots and service teams and such other organizations and facilities as were assigned or attached to the IX Air Force Service Command.

d. Formulation of detailed plans and publication of directions governing supply, assembly, repair, maintenance, modifications, overhaul, distribution, and salvage activities.

e. Supervision of training of all IX Air Force Service Command units and organizations and the operation of schools and facilities, as directed by the Commanding General, Ninth Air Force, for the instruction of technical personnel of all arms and services within the Ninth Air Force.

f. Coordination between the Ninth Air Force and civil and military agencies within the theater of operations on matters pertaining to supply, maintenance and such other administrative functions as were not organically within or specifically assigned to other agencies of the Ninth Air Force.

g. The issuance of such technical instructions pertaining to material, equipment and supplies of aircraft and their related equipment as were not covered by technical instructions from higher authority.

h. Preparation of estimates for funds as required by agencies and facilities of the IX Air Force Service Command, with the exception of pay rolls of military personnel and the supervision of funds so allocated.

i. Disbursement of all public funds for the Ninth Air Force.

j. The preparation for issuance by the Commanding General, Ninth Air Force, of technical directives, procedures and instructions covering supply, assembly, repair, maintenance, modification, overhaul, distribution, and salvage activities, other than those applying exclusively to IX Air Force Service Command.

k. The determination and maintenance of adequate levels of supply at all depots, agencies and service units under the command or technical control of the IX Air Force Service Command.

l. Transportation or arrangement for transportation of personnel, equipment and supplies of Ninth Air Force units in excess of capabilities of organic transportation facilities.

m. The disarmament and demobilization of German Air Force units as directed by Commanding General, Ninth Air Force.

n. The issuance of orders and instructions necessary to accomplish assigned duties and responsibilities.

o. Such other specific duties as might from time to time be directed by the Commanding General, Ninth Air Force, or higher authority. (IX Air Force Service Command, Organizational Manual, Memorandum 20–2, 20 February 1945.)

More than 50 types of units were incorporated into the command to discharge these functions effectively. The entire structure was based upon the framework of (1) Headquarters IX Air Force Service Command, (2) advanced air depot areas, (3) base air depot area, (4) air depot groups or tactical air depots, (5) service groups, (6) quartermaster truck groups and (7) air transport.

Command headquarters was organized on the premise that the command functioned as A–4 of the air force. Instead of the conventional staff section system service command centralized control of almost all types of subordinate units under four major operating divisions: Personnel and Training, Transportation, Maintenance, and Supply. This structure, rounded out by a special staff, required no basic reorganization during the war. The following changes, however, were made to meet new or increased functional responsibilities:

a. A disarmament division was established.

b. The Operations section, under Personnel and Training division, and the Plans section merged into a new Plans and Operations division. This division was created because Operations, the organization and movement of all subordinate units, required intimate cooperation with Plans.

c. A Special Training Section was operative during the command's most intensive period of activity.

The command achieved rapid, flexible coordination with Ninth Air Force by establishing headquarters as close as possible to air force administrative headquarters and by maintaining intimate liaison with air force A–1 on personnel matters; A–3 on matters pertaining to operations and training; and A–4 on matters of transportation, supply and maintenance. (When Ninth Air Force adopted the directorate system liaison was kept up with the appropriate director).

The command assigned a full-time liaison officer to Ninth Air Force Advanced Headquarters on the continent to relay information concerning the status of units and to expedite the accomplishment of special projects and the interchange of ideas and plans. IX Air Force Service Command also maintained close liaison with transportation, chemical warfare, engineer, ordnance, quartermaster, signal and fiscal sections at air force headquarters.

A similarly intimate relationship existed between service command and the other commands, particularly 9th Bombardment Division and the tactical air commands. In October 1944 it was decided at a meeting of the Ninth Air Force Directorate of Supply that representatives of the service command supply division would make weekly visits to each command to discuss particularly urgent and individual problems.

Except for a detachment which crossed the channel with the first fighter-bomber groups, IX Air Force Service Command did not maintain an advanced headquarters.

The Bradley Plan anticipated the need for subordinate area commands to supervise operation of the service units. In October and November 1943 two advanced air depot areas were created to operate as small task force headquarters, with a horizontal organization similar to service command; i. e., the divisional and special staff structures.

The planned function of the BADA was to serve as a base supply depot on the continent, to assemble aircraft and maintain personnel replacement depots and to discharge intransit functions for air force supplies. BADA headquarters was organized the same way as command headquarters.

Air depot groups and tactical air depots were organized under IX Air Force Service Command to perform fourth echelon maintenance and to stock and issue all types of air force supplies. The practice of assigning air depot groups geographically was very satisfactory for the command and technical control of service groups and operations under that system were more effective than they were when the AADAs commanded the service groups. However, when they were used in the exercise of such command air depot group headquarters had to be enlarged.

Performance of third echelon maintenance and supply was the responsibility of the service group. Service units which prior to November 1943 had been assigned to tactical units were assigned directly to the service command and continued so throughout the operational period. An early plan proposed the division of service groups into two independent organizations, each serving a combat unit. It was found more expedient, however, to maintain service group headquarters to direct two service teams. Direct administrative control of the service groups was first assigned to AADAs and later to air depot groups, both of which supplied the service groups and supervised them technically.

Mobile reclamation and repair squadrons were assigned to the service group to service aircraft which crashed or landed with battle damage away from their home base. These squadrons, which were initially developed by VIII Air Force Service Command, were also utilized by IX AFSC to assemble aircraft and gliders and to supplement the personnel of air depot and service groups. They proved particularly useful and valuable to the air force because of their flexibility and mobility, which enabled them to execute a great variety of emergency functions.

Quartermaster truck groups were assigned to a truck pool in preparation for high transportation demands, but the shortage of truck transportation remained a difficult and acute problem throughout the entire campaign. This was due largely to the inability of Communications Zone to fulfill its original commitment to deliver all supplies, both common issue and those peculiar to the air force, to dumps or depots within 40 miles of the units which required them.

Service command's air transport in Britain consisted of an air transport group, which provided transport for cargo and passengers; a ferry squadron, which flew combat aircraft from assembly and storage points to combat groups; and an air transport wing which controlled the two organizations and was directly under command headquarters. After the invasion these air transport functions were expanded to include operations on the continent and between the continent and the United Kingdom. In September 1944 all three units were taken from the command and assigned to USSTAF, which assumed responsibility for ferrying aircraft and transporting cargo and personnel for the Ninth Air Force. It allotted a limited number of aircraft to the IX Air Force Service Command, which organized a provisional transport group for small scale internal operations on the continent. Later a ferrying squadron was reassigned to the provisional group.

On 31 December 1943, the command had assigned to it 245 units with a personnel strength of more than 32,000. For the most part original units came from VIII Air Support Command and VIII Tactical Air Service Area Command. Four of 12 air depot groups were activated by the IX Air Force Service Command in the United Kingdom. Three service groups and 4 service squadrons came from the ZI.

Peak strength was reached in July 1944, when more than 62,000 sonnel in 439 units were assigned to the command. Air depot groups totaled 13; service groups, 23.

In November 1944 a number of units with personnel were transferred to the First Tactical Air Force (Prov). A personnel increase of 2,217 in February and March 1945 was caused primarily by transfer into the command of limited service personnel from the ground forces, a program which was considered highly unsatisfactory by service command, which needed, not combat-weary basics, but highly trained specialists.

IX Air Force Service Command was assigned many functions which were not specifically mentioned in preliminary plans. Among the principal special functions were: glider assembly, disarmament, aircraft modification, flying control, and PW stockade.

IX Air Force Service Command's participation in the Normandy invasion was planned operationally and administratively through the Ninth Air Force planning group in coordination with Supreme Headquarters, Allied Expeditionary Forces; 21st Army Group (British); 12th U. S. Army Group; and Headquarters, Allied Expeditionary Air Force. The complicated logistics problem introduced by tables of supply requirements for the Ninth Air Force was worked out by the IX Air Force Service Command. In May 1944 General Miller was succeeded by Brig. Gen. Myron R. Wood, who retained command throughout the balance of the war.

Beach parties of the intransit depot group were the first units of the command to reach the beaches. They landed on 7 June and immediately began to establish air force supply dumps. Quartermaster truck companies followed, loaded with landing material and, on 8 June, the advanced headquarters of the command landed.

Signal companies, Ordnance ammunition companies, service groups, and elements of numerous other service units followed shortly thereafter. On D plus 33 the first air depot group came ashore. Service units accompanied all tactical units which shifted their bases of operations to the continent. By 1 November 1944, the entire command was established on the continent.

The command's accomplishment from 1 October 1943 to 8 May 1945 may be seen in the following statistical summary:

Aircraft repaired		15,952
Aircraft modified		5,427
Aircraft assembled		1,775
Aircraft salvaged		2,133
Cargo transported by truck	tons	858,235
Personnel transported by truck		195,735
Aviation gasoline delivered	gallons	241,248,780

C. SUMMARY OF ORGANIZATION

It has been shown that basic planning for the use of tactical air power in the European Theater of Operations was generally sound. It has also been shown that the Ninth Air Force deviated from these plans to accomplish effective tactical air effort. In review, the modifications that were called for to insure the maximum effort are as follows:

1. The development of the tactical air commands was called for by the urgent requirement to maintain the closest possible liaison with the cooperating army counterparts. The TAC headquarters was almost invariably adjacent to the headquarters of the army with which it coordinated its efforts. This close association was necessary for immediate interchange of air and ground information and joint air-ground tactical planning. In the air planning the air commanders selected the air objectives and established the target programs. However, such selection was normally aided by consultation with ground com-

manders. The result of this collaboration is obvious from the extraordinary air-ground cooperative success that was achieved.

2. The War Department authorization of separate air defense and engineer commands was absolutely essential, in that attempts to exercise effective control of these operations through the staff at air force headquarters would not only have been excessively slow and unwieldy but grossly inefficient. The huge staff that would have been required to control those units would have destroyed the mobility of the air force headquarters and seriously interfered with normal operations.

3. Operations in general, throughout the European theater, were hindered by the fact that requirements frequently arose for change in functions and/or operating procedures in units, which, however well justified, could very seldom be reflected in authorized changes of tables of organization and equipment. It was found that tables of organization and equipment were generally too inflexible for major changes of function. In particular it was found that the original T/O & E's of the tactical air commands were inadequate and had to be augmented from such sources as the inactive IX Fighter Command and by stripping wings of personnel. Another major example was the case of instrument bombing units, where provisional activation, organization, manning, equipping, and training were undertaken and met at the expense of the operational effort. Requirements for weather reconnaissance were met in a similar manner.

4. The pitifully small allocation of reconnaissance units, both tactical and technical, which were made available in the accepted troop basis plans, detracted most materially from the full effectiveness of the tactical air effort.

5. There existed, throughout the war in western Europe, a serious inadequacy in the night striking force and extensive augmentation was considered necessary to put the Ninth Air Force on an effective 24-hour operational basis.

6. The allocation of truck and motor transport to the air force was generally not adequate to cope with emergency situations requiring immediate large-scale movements.

7. Air transport facilities, controlled by the air forces and its commands, were also seriously inadequate. Air force reliance on external air transport agencies did not work out at all satisfactorily. This was

especially evident in a mobile campaign where all types of transportation were at a premium and communications were overloaded.

8. Service and combat commanders were, in general, not fully acquainted with one another's specific mission and function and, consequently, did not derive the benefits that would have resulted from closer association and mutual understanding of capabilities, limitations and problems.

9. Battle tactics and techniques taught in the Zone of Interior were considerably and continuously altered during combat in the European Theater of Operations. Replacement crews frequently arrived in the theater without adequate training for their combat assignment. Consequently the tactical air force was required to establish elaborate training programs and schools within the theater. This training obligation materially detracted from the over-all operational effort which the tactical air force exerted against the enemy.

A fuller consideration of Ninth Air Force organizational changes, the necessity for deviation from the orthodox rules for organization and the consensus of staff and commanders' opinion concerning internal and external organization will be found in chapters IV and V dealing with conclusions and recommendations.

Chapter IV

CONCLUSIONS AND RECOMMENDATIONS: EXTERNAL

(Derived from an analysis of Ninth Air Force relationships with lateral and higher headquarters of the ground and air forces)

A. GENERAL

1. "Aviation in Support of Ground Forces"

ALTHOUGH FIELD MANUAL 31–35, "Aviation in Support of Ground Forces," was a useful basic guide in tactical air operations, much of its material proved to be obsolete in the course of the European campaign.

The fundamental terminology of the manual, for instance, is not only outmoded but inaccurate. The previous conception of air "support," which recurs constantly in FM 31–35, has been definitely superseded by the richer, more accurate conception of air "cooperation." Another obsolete term employed in the manual is "observation," which does not adequately convey the program of visual, tactical, photographic and artillery reconnaissance carried out in 1944 and 1945 by the tactical air force.

FM 31–35's treatment of the composition of a tactical air force is no longer correct or applicable. The basic assignment of bomber, interceptor, air support and air force base commands to a tactical air force was modified in the Ninth Air Force to provide for a bombardment division, three tactical air commands, an air defense command, an air service command and an engineer command. Such flexibility in the alignment of commands is not visualized in FM 31–35.

To correct these and other inaccuracies and inadequacies and to present a modern, complete doctrine for the employment of aviation in cooperation with ground forces, it is recommended that FM 31–35 be reviewed and revised on the basis of practical air-ground experience in the ETO and other combat theaters.

2. Control of Air Power

The eminent success of air power in the war of western Europe unqualifiedly proved that the striking power of the air forces must not be divided by assigning or attaching subordinate air units to elements of the ground forces. Such a division, which was not made in the ETO, would make it impossible to employ tactical air power with the greatest flexibility and effectiveness.

It is recommended that the equality and interdependence of air and ground forces be maintained as inviolable military policy, that direct control of all available air power be centralized under the air force commander and that the air force commander be responsible for operations directly to the Supreme Commander.

3. Troop Basis of the Original Organizational Plan

The original organizational plan (most commonly referred to as the Bradley Plan) for the tactical air force which would cooperate with the ground forces in the Allied assault on western Europe was basically sound and adequate in its troop basis, although certain deficiencies became apparent as the organizational plan began to take its physical shape.

The basic deficiencies were:

First, adequate provision was not made for personnel for the additional operational headquarters which the tactical air forces in the ETO required in order to cooperate with the 12th Army Group and its four armies and with the 6th Army Group and its one U. S. army. (Although it was advanced as the inclusive basis for the strength and organization of American tactical air power in the ETO, the planned troop basis applied only to the Ninth Air Force and did not anticipate the formation of the First Tactical Air Force (Prov)).

Second, adequate provision was not made for officer and enlisted personnel for tactical air liaison parties, air liaison officers, operational research and similar functions.

Third, adequate provision was not made for military police and security battalions to guard airdromes and other installations. (Most of the temporary airdromes which the Ninth Air Force occupied were inadequately guarded, and it was frequently impossible to prevent civilians and unauthorized military personnel from entering installations, pilfering equipment and interfering with military functions. The use of civilian guards was unsatisfactory because they usually did not speak English and did not understand the nature of their employment.)

Fourth, an inadequate allocation of basic enlisted personnel made it necessary to use technically qualified personnel for basic functions.

Fifth, no provisions were made for the personnel and equipment to organize the necessary instrument bombing units required in the all-weather conduct of operations.

Sixth, there were seriously inadequate provisions for all phases of reconnaissance—both tactical and technical. Example: No provision was made for weather reconnaissance.

Seventh, no adequate provision was made for night photographic reconnaissance. The entire allocation for the tactical air force consisted of one flight of personnel in a photo reconnaissance squadron. Another example: the minimum requirement of Ninth Air Force was five reconnaissance groups, but only two were provided, one of them a photo group.

Eighth, no provision was made for a training command.

Ninth, no provision was initially made for an engineer command.

Tenth, no provision was initially made for an air defense command.

Eleventh, decidedly inadequate provision was made for night striking forces of all tactical types.

Twelfth, decidedly inadequate provision was made for Ordnance maintenance companies for a highly mobile tactical air force.

It is recommended, in future planning for a tactical air force to cooperate with an army group, (1) that provision be made for ample bulk allotments of personnel to meet unforeseen requirements; (2) that provision be made for instrument bombing units, a weather reconnaissance agency and adequate tactical and technical reconnaissance units; (3) that the allotment of guard and security personnel be considerably larger than it was for the Ninth Air Force; (4) that provisions be made for the nucleus of a training command, an air defense command and an engineer command that could be rapidly expanded and equipped as dictated by the immediate tactical situation; (5) that thoroughly adequate provision be made for night striking forces of all tactical types; and (6) that the urgent requirement for mobility in a tactical air force be recognized by future air force planners by authorizing completely adequate air and motor transport and a large complement of Ordnance maintenance companies.

4. Requirement for Theater Air Headquarters and Statement of War Department Policy for Co-Equal Air-Ground Headquarters

There existed a need at theater level for separate, co-equal air and ground headquarters, which could closely coordinate their operations but remain independently responsible to the theater commander or the Supreme Commander, as the case might be. (See chart of proposed organization on p. 97.) In addition to coordinating theater-level air-ground administrative and operational planning, such theater air headquarters would establish over-all air administrative and operational policy and generally supervise its execution. More specifically, it would: (1) requisition and assign all air forces personnel; (2) establish for the several air forces uniform policies for combat crew replacement, rotation of personnel, leave quotas and furloughs involving extensive travel; (3) coordinate all matters between the air forces in the theater and headquarters army air forces; and (4) establish and maintain liaison with the various other Allied governments in the theater and branches of their armed forces.

If such operationally coordinated but independent air and ground theater headquarters had been maintained in the ETO, the resultant gain in flexibility of decision and promptness of action by the theater level of air command would have materially aided the Ninth Air Force in the execution of its administrative and operational commitments.

There further existed in this theater a requirement for a concrete War Department statement of policy as to which air and ground headquarters would be considered co-equal.

It is recommended:

a. That the War Department established co-equal air and ground theater headquarters, which would coordinate their operations but remain independently responsible to the over-all theater commander or the Supreme Commander, as the case may be. (See chart Page 97).

b. That the theater air headquarters be responsible for all AAF and theater matters of air policy determination and dissemination and for air liaison with other governments and branches of their armed forces.

SUGGESTED THEATER LEVEL ORGANIZATION

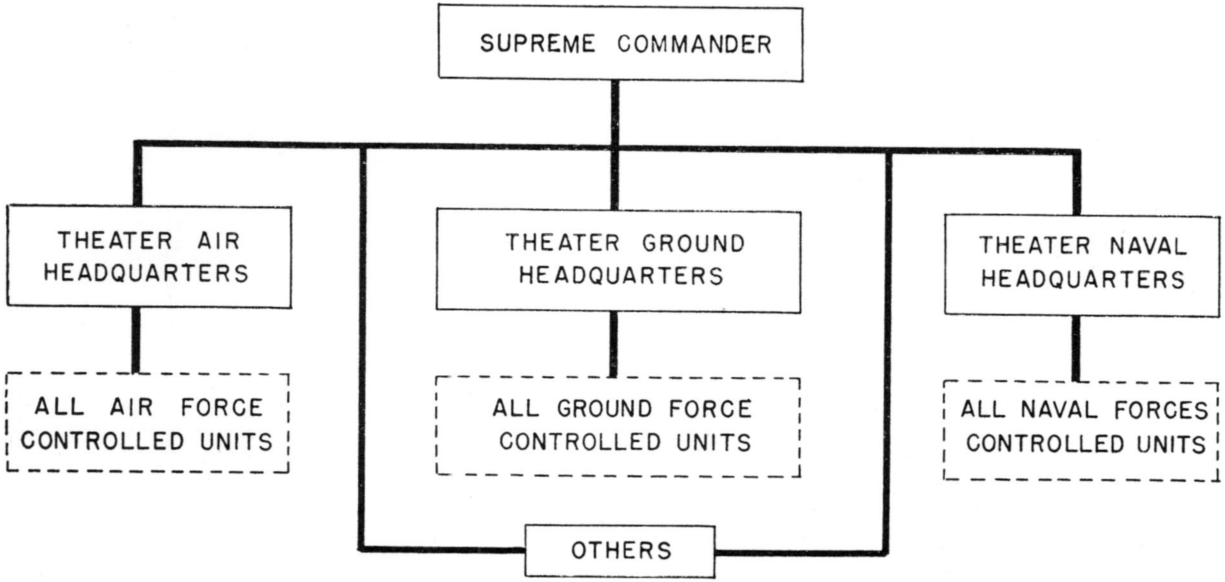

(Supply channels to follow conventional lines)

5. Authorized Representation of WD and Hq AAF in the Theater

Operations in general throughout the air forces in the ETO were hampered by the fact that, although requirements frequently arose for changes in functions and operating procedures of units, such requirements could very seldom be reflected in changes in unit authorization. The T/O & Es were generally too inflexible for major changes of function.

It is recommended that in future wartime operations the War Department and Army Air Forces establish in each theater representatives authorized, within broad policies established by the War Department, to approve special equipment lists (where the equipment required exists in the theater or in excess stock in the Zone of the Interior) and augmentation, activation, disbandment and establishment of units within the troop basis.

6. Comparative Rank—Air Forces and Ground Forces

The air force and its components were at a disadvantage in the European Theater of Operations, because the commanders of air components were of lower rank than the commanders of their associated ground components. Three of the four tactical air commands were commanded (originally) by brigadier generals, while their three associated armies were commanded by lieutenant generals. This disparity extended throughout the TAC-army staffs as well. Frequently air commanders and their staffs were required to deal with ground officers two grades higher but occupying comparable command and staff positions. This is not intended to imply that air-ground relations were not generally very amiable or that problems were not equitably worked out. However, differences in grade imposed considerable disadvantages on air components dealing with the ground forces.

If the air force had had a greater number of general officers in operational and administrative positions, smoother cooperation and planning with the ground forces could have been achieved.

It is recommended that officers in command or staff positions, for which existing T/Os authorize general officer grade, be favorably considered for promotion to the authorized grade. If the officer occupying the position is not qualified for general officer grade, he should be replaced by an officer who does so qualify.

It is further recommended that existing T/Os be amended to provide that air force command and staff officers be authorized similar grades to parallel ground force command and staff officers, where it is established that certain air and ground headquarters will cooperate on a co-equal basis.

7. Replacement Training

The combat tactics and techniques originally taught at training centers in the Zone of the Interior were considerably and continuously altered in combat. In the campaign in the ETO replacement pilots frequently arrived in the theater without adequate training for their combat assignments.

Consequently the tactical air force was required to establish elaborate training programs and schools within the theater, most specifically within the IX Air Force Service Command. This training obligation materially detracted from the over-all operational effort which the tactical air force could exert against the enemy, since no provision had been made in the troop basis for training on such a scale and therefore personnel and material needed in combat had to be allocated for training purposes.

Since combat tactics and techniques were invariably developed and modified in the theater of operations, it was felt that it would have been advantageous to have had an active liaison branch of the AAF Training Command established in each overseas theater to observe, study and implement the necessary training of replacement crews in the Zone of the Interior in the current tactical and technical developments learned in combat. Furthermore it would have been practicable and desirable to maintain a steady flow of highly qualified, experienced personnel to serve as instructors and/or advisors, either on temporary duty or permanent change of station status. It was further determined that provision should have been made in the basic troop basis of the theater air force for the nucleus of a training command which could have taken care of urgent training requirements which frequently arose in the various air components in the theater.

It is recommended:

a. That AAF Training Command established an active liaison office in the theater, with qualified observers to keep the training command in the ZI completely informed as to current operational training requirements.

b. That, if personnel cannot be adequately trained for immediate active participation in operations before departure from the Zone of the Interior, the Theater Air Force Training Command set up a training program in the combat theater in conjunction with the theater replacement pools, wherein tactics and techniques peculiar to the theater would be presented to incoming air and ground crews who have previously received sound basic training.

8. Basic Air Defense Doctrine and Policy

The basic doctrine on air defense, as stated in FMs 100–5, 100–15, 1–25 and 100–20, is essentially sound. Ninth Air Force experience indicated, however, that the doctrine should be enlarged to include the following principles:

a. That the air force commander in any theater is responsible for air defense in that theater and that he should delegate to his air defense and his tactical air commanders such responsibilities as are tactically proper to them.

b. That all AAA engaged in area air defense operations must be completely integrated into the air force air defense system, in order to attain maximum efficiency and minimum interference with friendly air operations.

c. That all air defense components, including antiaircraft artillery, should be assigned to the air force and further assigned or attached as required by the various using agencies within that air force's sphere of responsibility for air defense.

Controversy which arose between air and ground forces as to responsibility for control of AAA in certain areas would have been eliminated if there had been a War Department policy clearly delineating the responsibility of air and ground forces for defense from air attack. On the basis of experience in the ETO it is concluded that the air force must control all air defense weapons in the tactical air zone, except those automatic weapons units organic to ground units for close defense of their troops in the fighting zone.

Since complete coordination and control can best be attained if all elements of the air defense system are organized, trained and operated by the force basically responsible for air defense, it is recommended that *all* antiaircraft artillery (including short range weapons, currently of the automatic weapons type) be transferred to the air force and become a complete responsibility of that force.

Recognizing the requirement of ground force units in the ground fighting zone for short range AA weapons under their own control for the close defense of their units and transient installations, it is further recommended that the air force train units for this role and, during ground operations, assign such units to the ground forces.

9. Procurement, Screening and Dissemination of Intelligence

The superior air headquarters in the ETO did not assume the responsibility of surveying all external intelligence sources within the theater, screening these sources, making use of their materials and transmitting to the lower units all intelligence which would be useful in their operations. Lower units did not appreciate or understand that the responsibility for screening and exploiting external intelligence sources should normally be solely the function of the superior headquarters. The superior air headquarters staff must be large enough to encompass an evaluation staff of "professional" intelligence personnel, thoroughly versed in and devoted to their duties. The acceptance of such a function by the superior air headquarters would prevent the repetition of the situation which existed in the ETO, where a vast amount of uncontrolled intelligence was interchanged between subordinate commands. It would have further obviated the Ninth Air Force's direct dependency upon British agencies for the great bulk of its intelligence material.

It is recommended that the superior air headquarters in a theater be staffed to accept the responsibility for procuring, evaluating and disseminating to lower units all intelligence from external sources.

10. Intelligence Officers

The training of intelligence personnel which was undertaken by the Army Air Forces in the United States was found to be excellent in preparing officers for duty with the combat groups. It is felt, however, that there was a lack of trained intelligence personnel for duty in higher echelons. Many officers who were impressed into intelligence duties in commands and higher echelons had little knowledge of military staff procedure or of the functions and responsibilities of intelligence at those levels. It is felt that the service suffered by reason thereof.

It is recommended that the War Department establish a permanent intelligence school for the sole purpose of training intelligence officers for service with both air and ground forces. This schooling should include air, ground, naval and State Department intelligence as the basic curriculum. The highest caliber of regular air force officers and a certain top percentage of graduates of the USMA should be offered the intelligence service as a permanent, attractive career, with a liberal promotion policy as further inducement.

It is further recommended that the activities of the intelligence service be closely integrated with those of the Department of State.

11. Air Forces Class I, II, III, and IV Supply

Generally, under tactical conditions in the ETO, it would have been impossible for the air force economically to maintain Class I and III supply depots because they would have duplicated army and Communications Zone depots in the same areas. Furthermore, these supply items required daily issue and were too bulky to be easily hauled great distances, especially in view of the severe shortage in air force truck transportation.

The issue of Class II and IV supply items presented a special problem to the air forces in the ETO. When such supplies were adequate throughout the theater, the practice was for individual service teams to draw directly from Communications Zone and army supply points. However, when a critical shortage of these supplies developed, it would have been confusing and inequitable to allow service units to draw individually from the Com Z and army supply points. It was necessary that one air force agency, familiar with total air force needs, be responsible for drawing the issue for the entire air force and for distributing such issue equitably to all subordinate units. Consequently, during the period when Class II and IV items were critical, IX Air Force Service Command was employed as the centralizing air force supply agency which drew the entire allotment from Com Z and army depots and subsequently distributed these items to service teams and other air force subordinate units.

It is recommended that Class II and IV supply be obtained by one AAF agency in bulk and that it be stocked and issued by the air depot groups.

(NOTE.—Common-user items of engineer equipment should be an exception to this recommendation).

12. Requirement for Joint Air-Ground Traffic Priority Board

In theory, other agencies were to assist IX Engineer Command in moving its construction supplies. In practice, it was found that aid from outside sources was frequently negligible when it was most urgently required.

It was also found that the movement of troops and supplies in various joint air-ground operations was rendered difficult by the lack of a central traffic priority agency.

It is recommended that when the air force requires transportation in excess of its organic transport or when transportation bottle-necks develop, a joint air-ground board at air force-army group level be established to determine priorities of movement of personnel and supply.

13. Requirements for Theater Weather Service

Experience in the ETO demonstrated that when several weather squadrons operate within a theater a central agency should be established to coordinate policy, communications and supply. When combined operations are conducted with the military forces of other nations, it is believed that this coordination should be effected at theater air headquarters.

It is recommended:

a. That weather services and facilities be organized on a world-wide basis, with command of the various divisions within the theater exercised at theater air headquarters through a weather section.

b. That a mobile weather squadron be assigned to each tactical air force and that the staff weather officer of the air force normally should be control officer of the squadron.

c. That the control officer of the squadron also serve as weather officer of the army group with which the air force cooperates.

d. That there be appropriate subdivisions of the squadron at those levels on which coordination of requirements and action is best achieved.

e. That adequate provision be made for transmission of weather information by radio and landline communications, that radio communications personnel be assigned to the weather squadron and that the T/O & E include radio communications facilities.

f. That all weather personnel be assigned to the weather squadron (or similar organization) operating with an air force and its various components which require weather service.

14. Internal Combustion Engine Types

Considerable saving in time, cost and maintenance could have been effected by a reduction in the number of types of internal combustion engines used for such purposes as generating power for radars, radios, search-lights, lightings, wire communications, and engineer tools.

It is recommended that a survey be made of the requirements of all branches of the armed forces for internal combustion engines and electrical generating equipment, with a view to reducing substantially the number of different types of such equipment.

15. Experimental Photography

The Air Technical Service Command established an experimental photographic section in the ETO, which, through close liaison, was of inestimable value to the Ninth Air Force.

It is recommended that future air planning include at theater air forces level an experimental photographic section to assist in the development of photographic equipment required by tactical units.

Chapter V

CONCLUSIONS AND RECOMMENDATIONS: INTERNAL

(Derived from an analysis of the general internal organization and operation of the Ninth Air Force)

A. GENERAL

1. Tactical Air Command—Army Team

THE PRINCIPLE of establishing a separate, autonomous tactical air command to operate in an indissoluble operational partnership with each army proved sound and successful in combat. The intimacy of the TAC-army partnerships in the ETO and the variety of operational tasks which the TACs carried out independently in cooperation with associated armies demonstrated the effectiveness of this type of tactical air force organization. Perhaps the gravest inadequacy of the tactical air commands as they existed in the Ninth Air Force (see recommendations below) was the fact that they were not properly equipped to discharge the three phases of the tactical air mission 24 hours a day.

It is recommended that plans for joint air-ground operations provide for a tactical air command to cooperate with each army in the field and that each tactical air command be equipped to perform successfully the three phases of the tactical air mission 24 hours a day.

2. Operational Air-Ground Headquarters Proximity

On air force and tactical command level, and such higher levels as may be established, the air headquarters should be adjacent to ground headquarters. An immediate, on-the-spot interchange of air and ground information is essential. Planning must be conducted jointly, on an hourly or minute-by-minute basis if necessary, by the air and ground commanders and their staffs.

It is recommended that the closest physical proximity be maintained between air and ground headquarters from TAC-army level upward.

3. Air Ground Joint Planning

One of the major contributing factors in the success of the Allied campaign in the ETO was that from the outset operations were planned jointly by ground and air officers working in closest harmony. The air plan and the ground plan operationally and administratively formed an indivisible whole.

Phase 2 and 3 operations were carried out with the maximum tactical advantage when the objectives were considered jointly by air and ground. Selection of objectives and establishment of target programs were responsibilities of the air commander, but he benefited from consultation with his associated ground commander. Similarly the operations and objectives of the ground forces were determined by the ground commander, but it was to his interest to consult the air commander on the possible application of air power in coordination with particular ground moves.

In the ETO air and ground organization and policy permitted unbroken coordination in planning combined operations up to and including air force-army group level. This system was highly satisfactory and helped make possible the most powerful and effective application of tactical air power in history.

It is recommended that the principle that air and ground must be co-equal and interdependent remain inviolable and that the tactical air force emphasize and work toward complete cooperation in all joint operations.

4. Exchange of Air-Ground Personnel for Orientation

The Ninth Air Force initiated and maintained a program of mass air-ground liaison which went far beyond the conventional forms or the normal extent of liaison. Under this program, which was conducted in cooperation with the ground forces, thousands of air and ground officers and enlisted men visited parallel ground and air units. All available evidence indicates that this program was completely justified by its results. Air and ground personnel were impressed with each other's work. Air crews developed a keener sense of their responsibility and the capabilities of their weapons in combined air-ground warfare and ground forces personnel learned first-hand the extent, power and limitations of the air effort. The entire program improved morale in both services and increased good will and understanding.

It is recommended that air force and army group officially establish a program of exchange visits between ground and air personnel in parallel units and that the object of this program be mutual indoctrination and understanding. It is further recommended that this program be conducted in the peacetime military forces.

5. Tactical Bombardment Employment

Tactical bombardment power in the Ninth Air Force was not decentralized into small units controlled by the tactical air commands. The principal value of the tactical bomber was in the accomplishment of Phase 2 operations on a comprehensive scale ahead of the entire army group front. With its knowledge of the entire area of tactical responsibility, the air force alone was able to plan the most effective over-all employment of tactical bombers. It was recognized, however, that a definite requirement existed for a scale of bombardment effort equivalent to that of a medium bombardment group in each TAC. Such requirement may have been unnecessary if there had existed the necessary communications and control channels for instantaneous assumption of control of medium bombardment effort and the authorization from air force arbitrarily to assume such control.

It is recommended that the over-all control of tactical bombardment aviation be exercised directly by the air force and that such aviation be maintained as a single centralized striking force. It is further recommended that, either (1) the tactical air command be assigned one medium bombardment group or (2) adequate means for control and procedures be developed which will permit the TAC to call for prompt and effective application of other than its own bombardment power.

6. The Medium and Light Bombardment Combat Wing Headquarters

All Ninth Air Force medium and light bombardment groups were organized into combat wings which were under the administrative and operational control of a bombardment or air division. Each combat wing had three or four bombardment groups assigned but exercised only operational control of its groups. Administrative control was vested in air division headquarters. This system proved to be highly successful in tactical bombardment operations and the bombardment combat wings not only were necessary but it was felt that they were properly employed.

It is recommended that, when more than five groups of medium or light bombers are employed by a tactical air force, a bombardment or air division with two or more combat wings be established as the command and control headquarters under the air force. It is further recommended that the wing be employed exclusively as an operational headquarters and that administrative matters be channeled directly from the groups to the bombardment division.

7. Requirement for a Weather Reconnaissance Squadron

The organization and full utilization of a weather reconnaissance squadron contributed materially to the success of the 9th Bombardment Division's tactical operations. This squadron was organized on a tactical basis under the direct operational control of 9th Bombardment Division and governed its operations by the tactical needs of that division. Synoptic reconnaissance, on the other hand, was flown from bases in the United Kingdom, covering predetermined routes, by aircraft furnished by USSTAF and British Air Ministry. Synoptic weather reconnaissance was performed on a scheduled basis for general distribution and was not governed by immediate tactical considerations.

It is recommended that a tactical air force, a tactical bombardment or air division or an organization of similar size include a specially trained tactical weather reconnaissance organization under its direct operational control. It is further recommended that a specially trained synoptic weather reconnaissance organization be assigned to each theater under direct operational control of the highest weather organization headquarters in that theater.

8. Organization of IX Engineer Command

The Bradley Plan recommended that all engineer components of the tactical air force operate under the direction of a staff division in air force headquarters. This phase of the plan did not prove feasible. The Ninth Air Force established a separate engineer command early in its build-up and all engineer units received by the air force were assigned to it. This system of organization and procedure—with IX Engineer Command operating under the direct command of the air force commander—proved extremely flexible and successful in battle.

It is recommended:

a. That an engineer organization of the size of the IX Engineer Command (25,000 troops) operate as a separate air force command, employing regimental and brigade headquarters to control the basic work unit, the battalion.

b. That regiment and command headquarters maintain reserve pools of equipment for use at critical points.

c. That engineer command operate under the direct control of the air force commander.

9. Engineer Aviation Units

Engineer units directly serving the Ninth Air Force learned the operating characteristics and requirements of the air force and its subordinate units. As a result of this knowledge, they were qualified to locate, design and construct facilities which would prove efficient with minimum consumption of time and without wasted effort.

The air force, in turn, learned the capabilities and limitations of its supporting engineer units and confined its demands to absolutely necessary facilities. Waste of effort was avoided by eliminating all work which would divert engineering effort from projects employing their full effectiveness.

It is recommended that, when an air force is intimately associated with an engineer command, both make every effort to understand each other's capabilities and limitations, so that waste of time and effort may be avoided.

10. Signal Equipment and Aircraft for Engineer Command

The Ninth Air Force issued to IX Engineer Command signal equipment which vastly increased the effectiveness of engineer working units. It is not believed that this equipment would have been available had the engineers been pooled under the theater chief engineer. The same situation applied to aircraft which could be used for the transportation of supervisory personnel and for rapid reconnaissance of forward airfields.

It is recommended that engineers supporting a tactical air force be furnished sufficient signal equipment to maintain rapid transmission of instructions and sufficient aircraft to conduct reconnaissance of prospective airfield sites in the forward area.

11. Establishment of Air Defense Command

The economical and versatile employment of air defense weapons and equipment by a major air force can best be insured by the establishment of an air defense command. Antiaircraft artillery is then put under the direction of the air defense commander, who is charged with complete air defense and security and with providing navigation aids.

It is recommended that an air defense command be established as part of one of the major air forces in any theater, department, district or other military area.

(See recommendation entitled "Basic Air Defense Doctrine" under General (External), this chapter.)

12. Area of Air Defense Command Responsibility

The experience of this air force dictates that the air defense command, under the direction of the air force commander, should be responsible for AAF defense in all areas, except as noted herein and in "AAA under the Tactical Air Command" below, this chapter. It is recognized, however, that the experience of the Ninth Air Force does not necessarily reflect that of other tactical air forces.

It is recommended that a joint air-ground board be established by the War Department to study combat experience in air defense in the ETO and other theaters and to develop a concrete and consistent policy for the delegation of responsibility for AAA defense in all areas. This policy would include responsibility for AAA defense in port areas, communications zones, air force installations and army forward and rear areas.

The Ninth Air Force recommendation is that an air defense command, under the direction of the air force commander, be responsible for AAA defense in all areas except those protected by AAA attached to the ground forces. A suitable complement of AAA automatic weapons units should be attached to the ground forces to maintain the close defense of their own troops in the fighting area. The strength of this complement should be governed by the situation.

13. AAA Under the Tactical Air Command

The experience of the Ninth Air Force further dictates that the tactical air commands should be responsible for the air defense of their own forward installations and the forward installations and communications of the ground elements with which they are associated. To provide antiaircraft components for discharging this responsibility,

AAA units assigned to the air defense command should be attached for operational control to the TACs. Control of supply, administration and training of such attached units should remain with the air defense command. (For basic recommendation, see "Area of Air Defense Command Responsibility" conclusions and recommendations above.)

It is recommended that responsibility for active air defense, when tactical air commands operate in the same theater or in the same military area as an air defense command, be fixed as follows:

a. The tactical air command will be responsible for the active air defense of its own forward installations and the forward installations and communications of the ground elements with which it is cooperating, except for those installations and communications which are protected by the air defense components attached to and under the control of the ground forces.

b. The air defense command will be responsible for the active AAA defense in all areas except those defended either by the AAA automatic weapons battalions assigned to the ground forces in the fighting zone or by the AAA units attached to the TACs. The air defense command will be responsible for all active air defense in its area if and when the tactical situation requires fighter aircraft to be placed under its control.

c. A line of demarcation, known as the "air defense boundary," dividing the TAC and air defense command areas of responsibility, will be established from time to time by the senior air commander.

d. All AAA in a theater or similar area will be assigned to the air defense command, except a suitable component of automatic weapons assigned to the ground forces.

e. An AAA brigade headquarters and a suitable complement of other AAA units from air defense command will be attached to each tactical air command to meet the responsibilities assigned in (a) above.

14. Close Association of AAA Units With Air Force Units

The European campaign proved the value of conducting the pre-operational training of AAA units jointly with air force units. In airdrome defense it was found most effective to maintain a permanent team association between one AAA unit and one air unit (fighter group or bombardment group).

It is recommended:

a. That the air forces be responsible for the AAA defense of their own installations, wherever they are located.

b. That one AAA unit be teamed with one particular air unit for airdrome defense and that the AAA unit accompany the air unit in all movements from one airfield to another.

c. That such AAA units participate each year in an intensive joint training program with their associated air units.

15. Administration and Supply of Air Defense Command

The administration and supply of AAA units in the IX Air Defense Command during operations were not satisfactory, because these units had the ambiguous status of being assigned to Communications Zone and being attached to Ninth Air Force.

It is recommended that in the future the air force administer and supply its assigned or attached AAA components.

B. AIR FORCE HEADQUARTERS

1. Division of Headquarters

The division of Headquarters Ninth Air Force into two physically separate components—one primarily administrative, the other primarily operational—contributed to the flexible, unhampered conduct of mobile combat operations.

From a communications standpoint the division of air force headquarters permitted the economical use of the relatively small number of wire circuits available. The operational headquarters was located near the tactical commands, making the rapid provision and maintenance of direct and "hot" circuits a possibility, whereas the administrative headquarters, located in the vicinity of higher headquarters and supply and personnel sources, was in good communication with these units.

It is recommended that a tactical air force headquarters, cooperating with a rapidly moving army group, be so organized that it is possible to separate the headquarters into an operational and an administrative component when highly fluid tactical situations exist and that the former be charged with the absolute minimum of administrative functions consistent with efficient operation.

2. Air Force Headquarters Under Directorate System

Although the reorganization of Headquarters Ninth Air Force under the directorate system was not a perfect solution to all the organizational problems created by a swiftly changing tactical situation, it is felt that the advantages gained by the adoption of this system substantially outweighed the disadvantages.

The adoption of the directorate system gave general staff officer status to the Director of Reconnaissance and Photography and to the Director of Communications, for whom no such provision is made in standard staff organization.

The functional organization and the operating procedures of the advanced headquarters underwent only slight changes from the adoption of the directorate system to the end of the war in Europe. The fact that no major and few minor changes were required indicates the feasibility and soundness of the directorate system for a mobile tactical air headquarters. It is not intended here to imply that this is the only efficient way to organize a tactical air force headquarters but to point out that such an organization did function efficiently under operational stress in a war of rapid movement.

The employment of the directorate system of staff organization is recommended in situations where operational requirements dictate the division of an air headquarters into two components—one mobile and operational, the other administrative and relatively static.

3. Reorganization in Combat

During the continental campaign Headquarters Ninth Air Force was directed to reorganize under a T/O & E and to relinquish the use of air force manning tables and other bulk allotments of grades and ratings. If that directive had not been rescinded, the organization and the administrative and operational procedures of the headquarters would have been seriously disrupted. The entire flexibility of Advanced and Main Headquarters had been made possible by the use of manning tables and allotments.

It is recommended that organizations engaged in combat be free from T/O & E changes which they do not themselves request.

It is further recommended that the strength of air force and command headquarters be made adequate to permit flexibility in meeting sudden changes in the tactical situation and in personnel requirements.

4. Operational Coordination Between Air and Ground Staffs

Exceptionally effective liaison was maintained with army group by the establishment of an army liaison section consisting of the army group G–2 Air and G–3 Air staff sections physically within air force headquarters. This system was most effective and provided an expedient means for army group-air force cooperation. These two army group sections, directly responsible to the Commanding General, 12th Army Group, both administratively and operationally, although operating at Ninth Air Force Advanced Headquarters, furnished air planners the most current army group plans, cooperated in screening army requests for tactical bombardment effort, provided valuable target information and ground intelligence not available through air force channels and generally assisted coordination betwen air force and army group staff sections.

It is recommended that close operational liaison with army group be maintained by locating the G–2 Air and G–3 Air sections physically within air force headquarters and that these sections remain directly responsible to the Commanding General of the army group, both administratively and operationally, while working in close coordination with air force A–2 and A–3 during operations.

5. Duplicate Operations Equipment for Air Force and TAC Headquarters

It was essential that air force and TAC headquarters have duplicate operations equipment in order to maintain the continuity of the tactical air campaign and to prevent disintegration of the entire operational structure in the event that the headquarters is over-run by the enemy. The latter situation never developed in the ETO, but the danger was not always merely theoretical. During the German counter-offensive in the Ardennes advanced or operational headquarters were frequently in precarious positions and it was necessary for the rear or administrative headquarters to be ready to assume control of operations at any moment. In more routine circumstances—specifically during the movement of air force or TAC headquarters from one location to another—operations equipment had to be available at both sites to prevent any interruption in the centralized control of group operations.

It is recommended that in a mobile tactical air force whose headquarters may be engaged by enemy ground elements, duplication operations equipment be maintained both at rear and advanced headquarters and at the rear and forward echelons of advanced headquarters during moves.

C. PERSONNEL

1. Filler Replacements

During the first phase of the organization and training of the Ninth Air Force, the AAF practice of sending large shipments of casual personnel to the ETO proved generally satisfactory and did not impede the build-up of the air force. However, as the build-up period ended, this policy became impracticable and cumbersome. Considerable retraining and reclassification which should have been accomplished in the ZI was necessary in the ETO, simultaneous with extensive pre-invasion air operations. After the great influx of replacements for the initial build-up had ended, the air force wasted effort and experienced considerable difficulty in finding personnel with required MOS. Many officers and enlisted men with specialties not required in the ETO at the time nevertheless arrived there and it was frequently necessary to retrain and reclassify such personnel for new specialties.

It is recommended that policy governing the shipment of personnel to a theater of operations be based on a careful study of MOS required at each stage of development of the combat air force or air forces in that theater.

2. Replacement Pools

Replacement pools available in Britain and on the continent were used rather as holding organizations for casual personnel than as sources of replacements. Undesirable or unrequired personnel were occasionally placed in the pools and held for months awaiting disposition. Enlisted personnel in the grades of master sergeant and technical sergeant were sent from the ZI to the replacement pools in large numbers and assignments for men in such high grades were difficult to find. In some cases enlisted men in the first two grades were retained in replacement pools for as long as one year.

It is recommended that casual personnel awaiting assignment in replacement pools be held to a minimum, that personnel be dispatched from pools within 30 days of arrival and that highly qualified officers and enlisted men be assigned to operate these pools.

It is further recommended that only a certain closely controlled percentage of enlisted replacements in the first two grades be sent to a theater of operations.

3. Specialists

With the increased employment of specialized weapons and equipment by fighter-bomber and reconnaissance groups (for instance, rockets, large fragmentation clusters, pathfinder, oboe, radar, radar photography, AIBR, bombsights and other equipment and methods), the need for specialized test and check equipment and highly trained technical personnel increased considerably. In the final period of the campaign the Ninth Air Force experienced a severe shortage of such personnel and items of equipment.

It is recommended that such personnel and equipment be teamed in the ZI from the personnel-training period to the dispatch of both personnel and equipment to the combat theater or that the arrival of such personnel and equipment in a theater of operations be synchronized.

4. Flow of Replacement Crews

Ninth Air Force normally received information concerning the number of replacement crews expected in the theater sufficiently in advance for operational planning purposes. This information was promptly transmitted to the commands, which consequently had a realistic basis for crew and pilot replacement plans.

It is recommended that tactical air force headquarters be kept informed as to the anticipated flow of replacements so that sound and realistic policies for relief of combat crews can be established.

5. Rotation of Combat Crews

The system of combat tours based on a specified number of missions did not work out satisfactorily with respect to fighter-bomber or reconnaissance pilots. Combat personnel, who arrived in the theater with the knowledge that after a certain number of missions they would be returned to the ZI, were often impatient for the end of their tours. A rotation system for fighter-bomber and reconnaissance pilots based upon a specific period of time in the theater would undoubtedly be more satisfactory. The assignment of qualified combat personnel to staff duties when combat fatigue is evident is also considered desirable.

It is recommended:

a. That a flexible policy for rotation of combat crews on the basis of length of service overseas and intensity of combat operations be established.

b. That selected pilots whose combat efficiency had been impaired during the completion of a number of missions and who have shown an interest in the regular air force as a career be given a period of rest and recuperation, then be assigned to staff duties for an appropriate period, and finally be returned to combat flying duty.

c. That pilots suffering combat fatigue who have not shown an aptitude for or an interest in the regular air force as a career be rotated to the ZI.

d. That liaison pilots be rotated on the basis of length of service overseas. (It is suggested that the standard be 12 months of hazardous duty or 18 months of normal rear area flying.)

6. Rotation of Non-Combat Crew Personnel

The lack of a rotation policy for personnel other than combat crews resulted in unnecessarily long overseas service under arduous conditions for such personnel. By VE-day non-flying personnel assigned to Ninth Air Force usually had served overseas from 18 months to three years. This service involved intensive pre-invasion training, long hours of staff planning and, frequently, actual combat.

It is recommended that a rotation policy for non-combat personnel be established so that such personnel can be returned to the ZI for rest and recuperation after 2 years overseas service.

7. Decorations

In the European Theater of Operations there was no concrete and forthright policy governing the award of the Air Medal and the Distinguished Flying Cross. The several air forces awarded these decorations either for individual achievements of special merit or on the basis of participation in sustained operations. The latter basis, moreover, was not uniform among the air forces, certain of which awarded the decorations more liberally than others. This lack of uniform policy proved unfair to a number of flying personnel and caused a serious morale problem among the combat crews. As a result, both awards were devaluated and the Air Medal, in particular, was virtually reduced to the status of a "score card."

It is recommended that Headquarters, Army Air Forces, establish a concrete and well-delineated policy for the award of the Air Medal and the Distinguished Flying Cross in all theaters.

It is further recommended that the DFC be established as a decoration for distinguished flying, that its presentation, with rare exceptions, be restricted to pilots and that suitable decoration for distinguished airmanship be awarded to members of combat crews who are not pilots.

8. Battle Honor Awards

The theater policy governing the award of battle honors to ancillary units attached to or serving air force units proved inequitable, as indicated by inequalities in credit for redeployment and discharge. For example, units servicing combat groups were not awarded battle credits, while non-flying personnel of the combat groups were. Service personnel consequently felt that they had received unfair treatment. As another example the MTO did not have the same policy as the ETO with respect to the award of battle credits to air force headquarters and detachment personnel and members of ancillary units.

It is recommended that the War Department establish a clearly defined policy governing the award of battle credits so that uniform interpretation will prevail in all theaters of operations and for all types of units.

D. INTELLIGENCE

1. Intelligence Reports

During the relatively static tactical situation in the United Kingdom, there was a vast interchange of post-mission intelligence and operational reports between subordinate commands of the American air forces and the RAF. The communications network which carried this huge load of material was fantastic and should never have been permitted to develop. This deplorable situation continued to a limited extent even after the move to the continent.

It is recommended that higher headquarters assume the responsibility for assembling intelligence information from outside sources as well as its subordinate units and then distribute such information to its subordinate commands as is considered necessary or is specifically requested.

2. Post-Mission Reporting

A constant effort should be made to simplify reporting as much as possible and to reduce the number of required reports to a minimum. Urgent immediate post-mission reports should be made as brief as possible, so that communication lines can be free for other operational purposes. The Ninth Air Force transmitted detailed post-mission reports through normal messenger channels.

It is recommended that urgent post-mission reports be standardized on the highest level and that the standard form be employed by all air forces. It is further recommended that requirements of intermediate headquarters be treated as supplementary to the standard air force form and that in all instances wordage be reduced to a minimum.

3. Intelligence Publications

Considerable confusion and wasted effort resulted from the great flow of intelligence publications in the ETO. In an attempt to lead the uninitiated through the maze of publications, the Ninth Air Force A–2 Section published a guide to special publications and tried not to flood lower units with publications which would be of no use to them.

It is recommended that the highest air headquarters in the theater or similar military area receive and screen all incoming and available intelligence publications and transmit only such publications to subordinate units as are directly helpful for their planning, training and operations.

4. Aircraft Identification

Training in the recognition of friendly and enemy aircraft was greatly emphasized in the first phase of European campaign. The courses of instruction emphasized many insignificant differences between aircraft, many of which were experimental and outmoded types. The experience obtained in the aircraft recognition program indicated that it was sound and practical to eliminate all requirements for recognition except those aircraft which combat crews were likely to meet in the air. This curtailed recognition program resulted in a thorough familiarity with operational types of aircraft and did not overburden personnel with knowledge of many obsolete and infrequently contacted aircraft types.

It is recommended that aircraft recognition instruction be restricted to those types of enemy aircraft likely to be encountered in a theater.

5. Signal Intelligence

Although the signal intelligence organization of the Ninth Air Force rendered superior service, it would have been useless if it had not been able to operate with the large and experienced British intercept or "Y" service. Field units such as the Ninth Air Force organization were designed for tactical operations only and their work had to be supplemented by the more strategic rear area "Y" installations.

The "Y" service was an extremely valuable method of securing air intelligence for air defensive and offensive tactical purposes.

It is recommended that the air forces maintain a signal intelligence organization in war and peace, that this organization be engaged in active signal intelligence work at all times and that this type of work be developed continually from both a strategic and tactical standpoint.

6. Intelligence Communications System

It is recognized that a definite operational requirement existed for a communications system designed primarily to carry intelligence reports and messages. The necessary volume of flak intelligence, enemy air disposition information, reports of attacks on target and the many other intelligence items required in the air forces warrant the establishment or assignment of such communications. The use of radio in periodic net broadcasts is desirable. Such employment would normally eliminate the necessity for laborious relay of teletype messages emanating from air force headquarters down to the tactical groups.

It is recommended that the intelligence services in an air force be allocated a radio communications network and that it utilize radio net broadcasts to the maximum.

7. Photo Intelligence

The provision of trained photo intelligence personnel to the various intelligence agencies of the air force was entirely inadequate in basic air force planning. Fortunately, the need for such personnel was realized toward the end of the pre-invasion period and a sufficient number of personnel were trained hastily before D-day. However, the service rendered was initially sketchy and of relatively low standard.

It is recommended that a photographic intelligence section be established in Headquarters Army Air Forces to make a continuing survey of photo intelligence methods. This section should direct and supervise photo intelligence training, which should be made a significant part of the training of all reconnaissance pilots.

E. OPERATIONS, PLANS, ORGANIZATION AND TRAINING

1. Air Force Control of Tactical Air Operations

Delegation of considerable operational freedom by the Ninth Air Force to the bombardment division and tactical air commands was tactically sound and effective. Such delegation was necessary to maintain the required high degree of mobility for the air force's Advanced Headquarters and to permit the TACs to work directly and rapidly with their associated armies.

The large operations staff required to determine the many details of extensive tactical bombardment operations—including, for instance, the cancellation of projected operations due to weather—was retained at the relatively static headquarters of the bombardment division. Air force Advanced Headquarters, making only the major decisions as to the selection of targets and the weight and purpose of medium bombardment attacks, did not require this additional personnel and remained more mobile.

The tactical air commands presented a different situation, in that it is axiomatic that fighter-bomber operations must be very closely controlled by the tactical air commander through the TAC fighter control center and that the TAC itself must work very intimately with its associated army in providing close air cooperation. Thus the Ninth Air Force combat operations section, in its supervision of fighter-bomber operations, required only the personnel necessary for general supervisory control rather than for detailed close direction of daily air force operations. It must not, however, be assumed that air force control of fighter-bomber operations was or should be superficial. On the contrary, it was demonstrated repeatedly that the commander of a tactical air command, deeply engrossed in and intimately associated with the ground campaign, is subject to many strong influences to insure the maximum amount of close air cooperation in his area of responsibility at the possible expense of the proper employment of the air force as a whole in the combined air and ground battle. The proper employment of the air force as a whole requires sound and frequently redefined policies specifying the amount of fighter-bomber effort available for close cooperation with the ground forces and frequent readjustment of the number of fighter-bomber groups assigned to any one TAC to meet the changing tactical situation. Such re-definition of over-all policy and readjustment of available forces were, should and can only be determined by and accomplished at air force headquarters.

It is recommended, to reduce personnel and insure mobility at air force advanced headquarters, (1) that the combat operations section's control of tactical bombardment operations be limited to designation of targets, the weight and purpose of attacks and the units to provide fighter escort; and (2) that air force control of fighter-bomber operations, through the tactical air commands, be exercised by establishment of definite policies as to the allocation of forces available within the TACs to each of the three phases of tactical air operations, assignment of semi-permanent interdiction or airfield neutralization commitments, appropriate readjustment of the over-all force available to each tactical air commander and designation of relatively few daily targets or tasks, including bomber escort.

2. Mobility and Flexibility in Operational and Organizational Planning

The highest standards of mobility and flexibility were and must be maintained to achieve the maximum effectiveness of tactical air effort. All operational and organizational planning was and must be predicated on this principle.

It is recommended that operational and organizational planning in a tactical air force be strongly influenced by the necessity for preserving and augmenting the mobility and flexibility of this air force.

3. Application of Air Power During Static Ground Situations

In static tactical situations the Ninth Air Force devoted the major part of its effort to the maintenance of air superiority and to the isolation of the battlefield in preparation for the next offensive phase.

It is recommended that, when the ground situation is static or relatively static, the above principle be established as normal operational procedure.

4. Isolation of the Battlefield: Phase 2 Operations

The outstanding contribution of fighter-bomber aircraft, other than helping obtain and maintain air superiority, was achieved by assigning a large percentage of the available force to continuous armed reconnaissance operations to isolate the battlefield on the flanks and in front of the ground forces.

It is recommended that the doctrine of such employment of fighter-bombers be emphasized in the revised editions of FM 31–35 and all other War Department publications dealing with the application of air power in the ground battle.

5. Close Air Cooperation: Phase 3 Operations

The requirement for close cooperation operations was normally proportionate to and increased directly with the speed of movement of friendly lines or columns or the degree of fluidity of the front lines. When the front was relatively static, a greater portion of the tactical air effort had to and must revert to Phase 1 and Phase 2 operations.

It is recommended that this principle be incorporated in revised editions of FM 31–35 and all other War Department publications dealing with the application of air power in the ground battle.

6. Ground Direction of Aircraft to Targets

The direction of aircraft to targets by air force operations officers located with forward ground force elements was extremely effective. The weight of air effort thus exploited was closely controlled by the air commander.

It is recommended that the principal of ground direction to targets by air force operations officers operating in close coordination with ground force units be incorporated in planning for the tactical application of air power and for the basic organizational and equipment allowances of a tactical air command.

7. Armored Column Cover

One of the most successful achievements of the war in air-ground cooperation was the development by the Ninth Air Force of a system of close armored column cover by placing an air operations officer with ground-to-air communications among the foremost elements of an armored column.

It is recommended that the principle of ground direction of aircraft to targets by air operations officers in mobile control stations (tanks or armored cars, furnished complete with crew by the ground forces) be incorporated in planning for the tactical application of air power and for the basic organizational and equipment allowances for a tactical air command.

8. Tactical Air Liaison Officer Qualifications

For the most effective discharge of tactical air liaison duties, it was found that the TALO should be a field grade air officer with combat experience and with sufficient knowledge of staff procedure to function as an operations officer of the tactical air command. His essential duty was to evaluate mission requests for the TAC and to forward them to the TAC.

It is recommended that the tactical air liaison officer be a pilot with combat operations experience and with sufficient knowledge of staff procedure to serve as an operations officer of the tactical air command which he is representing.

9. Ground Liaison Officers With Air Units

The ground liaison officer system in the Ninth Air Force achieved highly satisfactory results. The practice of placing ground liaison officers with air units and air liaison officers with ground units was tactically sound and effective.

It is recommended that in future air-ground operations a liaison system be established whereby a suitable complement of air liaison officers will be placed with ground units and of ground liaison officers with air units.

10. Filtering of Army Requests for Close Cooperation

The filtering of army mission requests in the Ninth Air Force was performed first at TAC-army level, and it is believed that further delegation of such authority to lower units would result only in additional staff delay. The final decision as to whether or not army requests for air effort under TAC control would be fulfilled was made by the tactical air commander or his designated combat operations representative.

It is recommended that the tactical air command be the lowest command level to which authority for filtering, accepting and rejecting mission requests may be delegated.

11. Counter-Flak Fire

The effectiveness of fighter-bomber and medium or light bomber attacks on close-in targets was frequently increased by the carefully coordinated use of counter-flak artillery fire. With the tactical air liaison officer and G–3 Air of the cooperating ground unit working closely together before the air attacks, the ground forces fired on all known flak positions within range of and bearing on the target and frequently kept a "Cub" plane in the air during the attack to direct and adjust artillery fire to newly disclosed flak positions. When the target was out of the artillery range, effective counter-flak often could be directed against enemy flak positions on the route.

It is recommended that further effort and study be directed toward the development and perfecting of the system of using counter-flak fire in support of aircraft.

12. Bombers in a Tactical Air Force

The greatest capability of medium bombers was precision bombing of well-defined targets. This capability was most effectively employed and exploited in the air force's interdiction programs. The experience of the Ninth Air Force definitely demonstrated the need for tactical aircraft capable of achieving the results produced by the medium bombers. (There is no known reason why heavy bombers cannot be normally employed in a tactical air role if adequate airfields are available.)

It is recommended that basic planning for a tactical air force provide for a large complement of bombardment aircraft capable of precision bombing.

13. Provision for Precision Instrument Bombing

An agency capable of conducting precision instrument bombing through overcast must be an integral part of a tactical bombardment organization. The provisional pathfinder squadron, organized specifically for this purpose in 9th Bombardment Division, was given and discharged a tremendous responsibility. In months of bad weather, from 60 to 75 percent of the division's total effort could not have been made without the efficient operation of its pathfinder squadron.

It is recommended that an organization capable of conducting precision instrument bombing be developed and maintained at the highest possible efficiency as an integral part of the tactical air force.

14. Targets of Opportunity for Airborne Medium Bombers

During the campaign it was believed that a close radio liaison system between the TACs and the bombardment division, monitored by the air force, would have permitted an effective diversion of specific forces of medium or light bombers on the basis of TAC/R observations. Certain factors which were significant in medium and light bombardment operations—such as variable weather, the necessity for following carefully selected flak corridors and the higher percentage of larger-caliber bombs (1,000 or 2,000 pounds) carried by the mediums—could not be reconciled with the need for diversion.

It is recommended that studies be conducted by AAFSAT or a similar tactical research board or committee to develop the possibility of diverting bombardment aircraft to targets of opportunity.

15. Inadequacy of Night Striking Forces

The night striking force of the Ninth Air Force was inadequate. Extensive augmentation was considered necessary to put the tactical air effort on a real and effective 24-hour-a-day basis. Night bombing and intruder operations form a necessary complement to daylight fighter-bomber activity. This necessity was especially acute in the ETO, where the enemy largely carried out his movements at night and generally went unhindered because of the small available night force.

It is recommended: (a) that each tactical air command have a night fighter component basically trained and equipped for both night fighter and night intruder operations; (b) that a minimum force equivalent to approximately 25 percent of the day bomber force be trained and equipped to conduct night bombing and normally participate only in night operations; and (c) that each tactical air command have a component of bombardment-type aircraft for night intruder and night bombing operations.

16. Coordinated Control of AAA

The great variety and complexity of rigid flying restrictions in the ETO proved confining both to pilots and to ground AAA personnel. Close study of the development of a substitute system, which would be effective but less restrictive, is considered necessary.

It is recommended that coordinated control be substituted for inflexible flying restrictions in vital areas where heavy concentrations of AAA are located.

17. Combat Crew Training

The establishment of a training center outside of the bombardment division for training combat crews in theater techniques and tactics was determined to be more satisfactory than the maintenance of training programs within the groups. The groups normally were fully occupied with the conduct of operations and the maintenance of combat efficiency. They had a tendency either to slight the task of training replacements or to treat it too casually. Similarly, the pressing urgency of operations detracted from the quality of training within fighter groups.

It is recommended that a continuous study of the training requirements of each theater of operations be made and that pilots and combat crews be trained accordingly before shipment to the theater.

(See recommendation entitled "Replacement Training" in General (External), chapter IV).

18. Headquarters Administrative Type A/C Allotment

The air force headquarters administrative type aircraft allotment was completely inadequate for a mobile tactical air force which maintained two headquarters and which operated in countries where rail and road facilities had been reduced enormously by war.

It is recommended, on the basis of Ninth Air Force experience, that where dual headquarters are necessary the air force headquarters flight be augmented to include six C-47, six C-45, and six Cub airplanes or comparable types as the minimum number of administrative type aircraft authorized.

19. Movement Authorization Within the Air Force

The movement of Ninth Air Force units was based on current and future plans for movement submitted by the commands but was carried out only after authorization from air force headquarters. This centralization of movement control was essential in the ETO because of the structure of the Ninth Air Force and the nature of its association with lateral and superior headquarters. In the Ninth Air Force projected movements could not be finally authorized at a lower level than air force for external and internal reasons. The basic external reason was that the movement of air force units was necessarily governed by current and future planning at air force-army group level, in line with the broad directives of the Supreme Commander and administrative policies of the CG, USSTAF. Internally, unit movements often involved several commands and coordination was only possible at air force level. For instance, the movement of tactical units depended upon the ability of IX Engineer Command to construct facilities and of IX Air Force Service Command to stock and maintain supplies at new airfields and depots. Furthermore, the movement of tactical air command units frequently had to be coordinated with adjacent TACs. In movement, as in certain other matters which involved the several commands, the air force normally functioned as the coordinating and controlling agency. Finally, the shortage of transport throughout the Ninth Air Force made it necessary that movement priorities and schedules be established and authorized by a central agency at air force headquarters, to insure maximum economy and efficiency in the utilization of available transportation. In the ETO a broad general directive was used to control IX Engineer Command movement and this method sufficed. However, close supervision was maintained over all engineer command redispositions.

It was normal operating procedure within the Ninth Air Force for subordinate commands to prepare current and future plans for movement within their sphere of responsibility, which were submitted to the air force movements control section for coordination and phasing with other air force, army group and command plans.

On the basis of its experience in the ETO, the Ninth Air Force recommends that the various commands in a tactical air force prepare current and future movement plans, to be submitted to the air force movements control section for coordination and phasing in with other air force, army group and command movement plans.

It is further recommended that authorization for movement of subordinate units be maintained as an air force headquarters function in all air forces which are required to maintain a degree of mobility comparable to that of the Ninth and which have similar commitments for cooperation with an army group.

20. Desirability for Close Relationship of Combat Operations, Flak and Target Intelligence Sections

The closest possible relationship must exist between the flak, target intelligence and combat operations sections. The chief of each must attend all target conferences and briefings, become intimately familiar with all major recurring targets, keep abreast of the changing tactical situation and its bearing on the target and flak situation, and definitely realize that only through this tri-partite team can the air force be employed in the most effective manner. This also applies to the weather section, but to a somewhat lesser degree, because weather information guides the selection of target areas rather than the selection of the targets themselves.

It is recommended that the combat operations, flak and target intelligence sections at all times work in the closest physical and professional relationship.

21. Separate Combat Operations Section

Administrative separation of the combat operations section from the A–3 section was sound and permitted concentration on the vital task of conduct of Ninth Air Force combat operations. This would not be desirable in a peace-time organization.

It is recommended that for the actual conduct of air operations against the enemy a combat operations section be established administratively separate from and independent of all other functions normally performed by the A–3 section.

22. Establishment of the Operational Research Section

The organization and establishment of an operational research section in the air force was completely justified. It proved to be a particularly valuable service with regard to the use of new types of equipment and as an aid in the development of combat technique and tactics. In peacetime operation, however, there will be no need for a separate section at air force level. Research functions will continue in peacetime operations, but it is considered that the small-scale effort could be more efficiently handled in a small sub-section under A–3.

It is recommended that the physical part of research in a campaign should be carried out at command level, where it is in closer proximity to the target areas, and only over-all supervision and coordination exercised at air force level. The same situation exists in operational research (civilian), where only supervision should be exercised at air force level.

23. Supervision of Operational Research Activities and Reports

All operational research reports should be submitted to the Commanding General or his designated representative for final approval in order to insure that the contents are factual, that the recommendations are in accordance with air force policy and that the procedures suggested or recommended are in accordance with over-all air force planning and strategy.

It is recommended, in order to prevent possible misrepresentations of air force tactics, techniques and policies by militarily unqualified technical civilian personnel, especially in view of the world-wide distribution of operational research section reports, that all such reports be reviewed and approved by the Commanding General or his designated policies established by him.

F. SUPPLY, MAINTENANCE AND TRANSPORT

1. Air Force Supply and Maintenance Section

The Director of Supply (A–4) in Headquarters Ninth Air Force, after completion of the planning for and the beginning of Operation OVERLORD, acted in an advisory capacity to the commanding general and supervised the execution of arrangements pertaining to Services of Supply matters.

It is recommended that the supply and maintenance section of air force headquarters be headed by the Assistant Chief of Staff, A–4, with special staff sub-sections of the various service branches under his supervision. The functions of the Assistant Chief of Staff A–4 would include, in addition to his advisory duties, the establishment of all supply and transportation priorities between the commands; the establishment of supply policies as they affect the air force as a whole; approval of equipment required over and above T/E; allocation of aircraft; issuance of directives as required by action of higher headquarters; and representing the CG at all times on matter of supply in line with policies established by him.

2. Combat Commander—Service Commander

Service and combat commanders were, in general, not fully acquainted with one anothers' specific mission and functions. Consequently they did not initially derive the benefits which would have resulted from closer association and mutual understanding of capabilities, limitations and problems.

It is recommended that associated service and combat commanders maintain close liaison and work out all mutual problems in the early stages of training or of preparation for operations.

3. AADA Versus Air Depot Group System of Operation

The elimination of the advanced air depot areas did not impede or disrupt the operation of the IX Air Force Service Command. In fact, the closer relationship thus established between service command headquarters and the air depot groups resulted in smoother operation. The practice of assigning air depot groups to particular geographical areas was very satisfactory for the command and technical control of service groups, and operations under that system were more effective than they were when the AADAs commanded the service groups. The air depot group generally was an excellent medium for the command of service groups. However, when they are used in the exercise of such command, air depot group headquarters should be enlarged.

It is recommended that the air depot group headquarters be augmented sufficiently to handle the administration and supervision of a minimum of four service groups, special.

4. Service Group, Special, Versus Service Group

The Service Group, Special — a consolidation into three units of the seven units which comprised the old service group, plus three additional units to perform station housekeeping and administrative functions—is a compact and well-integrated unit. This unit was organized on the basis of lessons learned in combat but was not actually used in combat, due to the lateness of reorganization. However, it is believed that the increased utility of the service group, special, more than compensates for the loss of a certain degree of organizational flexibility.

It is recommended that the service group, special, be adopted as a standard Army Air Forces service organization.

5. Assignment of Service Group, Special

In the Ninth Air Force service groups which operated with tactical groups were assigned, controlled and administered by IX Air Force Service Command. The control exercised by the tactical group commander over a service group was limited to such administrative control as was required by his position as "station" commander. Tactical commanders have recommended that service groups be assigned to tactical commands, but this type of operation has not been tried by this air force and therefore such assignment cannot properly be recommended here.

It is tentatively recommended that service groups remain assigned to the tactical air force service command in a mobile tactical air war. However, it is further recommended that this question be made a matter of careful study at Headquarters AAF level, in order to determine the best method of assignment or even the possible integration of the tactical and service units into one self-sufficient unit.

6. Utility of Mobile Reclamation and Repair Squadrons

Mobile reclamation and repair squadrons gave IX Air Force Service Command a flexibility which it otherwise would have lacked. These units, self-sufficient even when divided into small detachments, were employed for many diversified purposes.

It is recommended that future tactical air force troop bases contain an adequate number of mobile reclamation and repair squadrons.

7. Inadequacy of Truck and Motor Transport in Air Force

The assignment of truck and motor transport to the air force was generally not adequate to cope with emergency situations. Shortages were felt most severely for the following reasons:

a. The rapid movement of units and the resultant necessity for long hauls very often required transportation of supplies several times the planned distances.

b. The exceptionally poor road conditions on the continent increased the time required for round trips over the supply routes.

c. For a considerable period gasoline had to be hauled from Cherbourg and the beaches to fields or dumps to the north and east of Paris before rail transportation finally became available.

d. The necessity for moving vast tonnages of construction equipment was not fully considered in pre-invasion planning. Consequently, IX Engineer Command was weak in transportation.

It is recommended, in order that the air force have sufficient transport to cope with the tactical and supply situation, that:

a. The air force be allocated sufficient ground and air transportation to maintain its own supply system over distances of 100 miles instead of 40 miles, as was the case in the ETO.

b. The air force be allocated an adequate number of 25- and 40-foot trailers and that 4-5 ton tractors be supplied to haul the large trailers.

c. Ordance sections of all T/Es be reviewed to eliminate unnecessary vehicles and to increase the allotment of 6 x 6 trucks.

d. Aviation engineers be furnished engineer dump truck companies at the rate of one per four battalions and Ordnance maintenance companies at the rate of one per eight battalions.

8. Requirement for Two Drivers Per Vehicle in Truck Companies

The pooling of truck companies into battalions and regiments proved particularly beneficial, in view of the widely-felt shortage of this type of transport. The combat training given truck company personnel moving to the continent in the assault phase was successful and the strengthening of these companies to maintain two drivers with each vehicle was entirely justified.

It is recommended that the T/O of truck companies be augmented to provide two drivers for each vehicle and that limited combat training be given truck company personnel operating in or near the frontline areas or in hostile territory.

9. Air Transport Shortage

The air transport facilities directly controlled by the air force and its commands were acutely inadequate. The movement of supplies would have been accomplished with more efficiency and speed if considerably more air transport had been provided as an integral part of the air force. Truck and rail transport was often excessively slow. It is not sufficient to provide an air transport agency to which the air force must apply for air lift, because in a mobile campaign with overloaded communications and all types of transport at a premium reliance on external agencies proves unsatisfactory.

It is recommended that provision be made for increased air transportation integral to the tactical air force, to be used for the movement of tactical air force supplies and units in fluid tactical operations.

10. Utilization of Air Force Beach Detachments

Considerable difficulty and confusion were avoided in the beach phase of Operation OVERLORD by the location of special detachments on the beaches to expedite the movement of air force supplies and operate air force dumps.

It is recommended that in amphibious operations air force beach detachments be established to handle air force supplies and operate air force dumps and that such detachments be attached to army engineer special brigades for training and experience before actual operation.

11. Chemical Maintenance Company in Air Force

The Ninth Air Force found it difficult to obtain chemical equipment maintenance facilities from ground and service forces.

It is recommended that at least one chemical maintenance company be assigned to the air force to make repairs and to assure a dependable supply of spare parts without recourse to other units.

12. Photographic Supply and Repair

Standard methods of obtaining photographic supply and handling photographic repair did not prove satisfactory in Ninth Air Force tactical operations.

It is recommended that a central specialized depot be established within the tactical air force for the purpose of handling supply of all photographic material.

G. RECONNAISSANCE AND PHOTOGRAPHY

1. Requirement for Separate Reconnaissance and Photo Section

The Ninth Air Force established a separate reconnaissance and photographic staff section which coordinated and supervised all reconnaissance and photographic activities within the air force. This section was directly responsible to the Deputy Commanding General, Operations, and closely coordinated its work with the Director of Operations, the Director of Intelligence, and the G–2 Air section. Under this system reconnaissance and photographic supervision was more efficient than it would have been under the Director of Intelligence and the Director of Operations. The establishment of a separate section made the conduct and administration of a highly technical phase of aerial warfare the responsibility of an officer specially trained in that field.

It is recommended that a reconnaissance and photographic section be established, in both the peacetime and the wartime organization of an air force, as a separate staff section.

2. Reconnaissance Allotments to a Tactical Air Force

Reconnaissance as organized and employed by the Ninth Air Force achieved exceptionally high standards of proficiency and efficiency in the campaign in western Europe. Reconnaissance was a most valuable source of information through photographic and visual observation of enemy movements and installations and bomb damage in rear areas and through provision to the ground forces, when weather permitted, of daily basic coverage of the battlefield. Reconnaissance also considerably increased the effectiveness of artillery by aerial adjustment. Reconnaissance under the TACs was essential to the proper functioning of the air-ground team.

It is recommended that one reconnaissance group be assigned to each tactical air command operating in cooperation with an army.

3. Need for Reconnaissance at Air Force Level

The speed with which requests for reconnaissance from air force, army group or higher headquarters were discharged was often seriously limited by the fact that the TACs required the entire resources of the reconnaissance group assigned to them. It was determined essential that a tactical air force headquarters have an assigned reconnaissance group consisting of an appropriate number of "all-purpose" reconnaissance squadrons, a night photo reconnaissance squadron, an appropriate number of light-plane reconnaissance units of the Cub type and a radar reconnaissance squadron. Experience in the ETO indicates that a minimum daylight effort equivalent to that of two "all-purpose" reconnaissance squadrons is necessary.

It is recommended that future planning for a tactical air force troop basis include a reconnaissance group to be assigned for air force-army group level reconnaissance. This group should normally have two or more "all-purpose" reconnaissance squadrons, a night photo reconnaissance squadron, an appropriate number of light-plane reconnaissance units of the "Cub" type and a radar reconnaissance squadron.

4. Night Photo Reconnaissance Requirement

The small night reconnaissance effort available to the Ninth Air Force detracted from the full effectiveness of the tactical air effort. Night reconnaissance was restricted by a complete lack of sufficiently trained units and a shortage of units which could be converted to night reconnaissance operations. The Ninth Air Force could have employed most profitably one night photo reconnaissance squadron for each tactical air command, as well as a squadron at air force headquarters.

It is recommended that each tactical air force headquarters and each tactical air command headquarters have an assigned night photo squadron.

5. Need for a Photo-Interpretation and Reproduction Center

The system of maintaining a photo-interpretation and reproduction center, with responsibilities divided between two different types of air force (the strategic Eighth and the tactical Ninth), was unsatisfactory. The Ninth Air Force at all times urgently required its own photo-interpretation and reproduction center, equipped and manned to:

a. Accomplish detailed and second-phase interpretation of photographs received from all aerial photographic units within the air force.

b. Issue target and special reports based on photographs received from all aerial photographic units within the air force.

c. Maintain a film and print library of all photographs within the air force.

d. Furnish quantity reproduction for air force units by both lithographic and photographic means.

e. Provide enlargements, mosaics, and other specialized photographic services.

It is recommended that each tactical air force be assigned a photo-interpretation center.

6. Gun Camera Film Processing

The experience of the tactical air commands demonstrated clearly the desirability of adding a well-equipped gun camera processing unit to each TAC for the rapid handling, processing, and assessment of gun camera film. The most effective way of employing such units would have been to divide them into detachments, one attached to each tactical group.

It is recommended that a gun camera processing unit be included in the troop basis for a tactical air command. The T/O & E of this unit should be augmented sufficiently so that detachments of the unit could be placed with each tactical group.

7. Integration of Reconnaissance and Photo Sections

It has been noted that planning and thinking at Headquarters, Army Air Forces, indicates that photographic staff sections and reconnaissance staff sections at various levels should be independent of each other. Experience in the ETO indicates the necessity, in a tactical air force, for complete integration of all photographic and reconnaissance staff functions under the reconnaissance staff section. Supply and utilization of photographic equipment for purposes other than reconnaissance, if not closely supervised and directed by one technically qualified agency, can seriously handicap the flow of photographic equipment and supply to reconnaissance units.

It is recommended that the tactical air force headquarters and the headquarters of its commands integrate the photographic and reconnaissance staff functions within their headquarters under the reconnaissance section.

H. COMMUNICATIONS

1. Signal Consideration in Headquarters Siting

The Signal Officer, Ninth Air Force, was always consulted, as far as practicable, in advance of a proposed relocation of the air force headquarters. His recommendations as to the suitability of proposed headquarters sites were carefully considered, with the result that communications to the new headquarters location were always adequate to continue efficient operations.

It is recommended that signal officers be advised of contemplated headquarters movements as early as possible and that the recommendations of the signal officer as to the suitability of new sites from a communications standpoint be carefully weighed before the final decision is made.

2. Signals and Communications Organizations

In the main, the signal and communications organizations authorized the Ninth Air Force were adequate for accomplishing the tactical mission. There were, however, certain important shortcomings which had to be overcome by special authorizations of personnel, special equipment projects and the creation of composite or provisional units.

It is recommended that, with the adjustments noted below, future tactical air forces be organized generally on the troop basis authorized the Ninth Air Force for signal and communications units. (The troop basis, of course, must be modified to meet special tactical problems, insofar as small special-purpose units, such as signal operations detachments and air-transportable radio teams, are concerned.) The following major adjustments in the troop basis authorized the Ninth Air Force for signal and communications organizations are recommended:

a. Augmentation of the signal service battalions assigned to air force headquarters by:

(*1*) A repeater team of approximately 24 enlisted men.

(2) A motor messenger team of 28 vehicles and 40 enlisted men.

(*3*) A VHF/FM radio company of approximately eight officers and 200 enlisted men.

(*4*) A wire construction team of 15 to 20 enlisted men and at least two K–43 line trucks.

b. Revision of T/O & E 1–547 dated 18 October 1943 to provide sufficient personnel and equipment to cooperate effectively with the armies in furnishing tactical air parties.

c. Furnishing each tactical air division (medium and/or light bombers) with a fighter control squadron or similar organization to install, maintain and operate the vast VHF "fixer" system required, as well as the ground stations for navigational and bombing aid devices.

d. The allocation of the following signal construction troops to a tactical air force:

(*1*) Per air force headquarters:

(*a*) One cable splicing battalion.

(*b*) Two heavy construction battalions.

(*c*) One light construction battalion.

(2) Per tactical air command:

(*a*) One heavy construction battalion.

(*b*) One light construction battalion.

(*3*) Per air force service command, air defense command and bombardment or air division:

(*a*) One light construction battalion.

e. Revisions of existing tables of organization to provide a minimum of:

(*1*) Five cryptographers per fighter or reconnaissance group.

(2) Two cryptographers per engineer aviation battalion.

(*3*) Three cryptographers per engineer aviation regiment.

(*4*) Eight cryptographers per signal company wing.

(*5*) Twelve cryptographers per signal battalion separate (TAC).

f. Integration of the aircraft warning and voice radio intercept control systems into a single organization.

3. VHF Radio for Medium and Light Bombardment Aircraft

In the Ninth Air Force VHF radio equipment was used in all medium and light bombardment aircraft in place of the HF radio sets normally installed. The advantages of VHF were simplicity of operation, greater reliability, more rapid communication and more accurate fixing and homing. Furthermore, the installation of VHF equipment in bombardment aircraft provided direct communication with escorting fighters and with the ground control systems of the tactical air commands. Normally the VHF communication range was sufficient to meet all requirements of medium bombardment aircraft.

It is recommended that all medium and light bombardment aircraft be equipped with VHF radio equipment.

4. "Y" Service

The signal intelligence or "Y" service in the Ninth Air Force was provided by the 3rd Radio Squadron Mobile (G).

It is recommended that an organization similar to the 3rd Radio Squadron Mobile (G) (less voice radio intercept detachment incorporated into the tactical control group) be provided each tactical air force and that detachments be maintained at each tactical air command and the air defense command.

(For further recommendations, see recommendation on signal intelligence in 4 B "INTELLIGENCE," this chapter.)

I. AIR INSPECTOR (Special Staff)

1. Tactical Air Force Inspection System

The system and organization of inspection in the Ninth Air Force were sound in principle. The entire air force received maximum benefit, with minimum interference and irritation to the inspected units.

On the basis of the experience of the Ninth Air Force in the ETO, it is believed that an inspection system for an air force of the size and composition of the Ninth Air Force should include:

a. Inspection by qualified station or unit inspectors at unit level once every 30 days.

b. Detailed inspection of units by a team of tactical, administrative and technical inspectors during each four-month period and interim visits of observation to follow up on recommendations made during the detailed inspection and to maintain supervision during changing conditions.

c. Sufficient detailed inspections to give first hand information on the efficiency of subordinate units and the manner in which commands are carrying out their responsibilities. (This information can best be gathered by inspections of command headquarters and a representative number of subordinate units.)

d. Supervisory inspections designed to insure that subordinate units maintain adequate and efficient inspection sections and fulfill their inspection obligations.

Inspections in all echelons should be conducted by a team of technical, administrative and tactical inspectors in order to reduce the number of different inspections and to secure thorough coverage during one visit. Detailed inspections of units at 4-month intervals should be the responsibility of the command headquarters which has administrative control over the units. Inspection reports should be routed from the unit inspected through the wing to the command so that the wing commander is fully aware of the efficiency of his subordinate units and can order staff visits to correct deficiencies.

It is recommended that no changes be made in the inspection principles and directives issued by higher headquarters upon which the above system is based.

J. PUBLIC RELATIONS (Special Staff)

1. Requirements for Ground Photo Units Assigned or Attached to PRO Section

Experience in the European Theater of Operations demonstrated that:

a. The public relations ground photography program should be conducted separately from the activities of various base photo sections.

b. Public relations cameramen should be trained news photographers, specially indoctrinated in the requirements of air force news photography.

c. The air forces should have photo units similar to those of the ground forces, with mobile dark rooms, courier facilities and all necessary equipment to produce a comprehensive pictorial story and to send photographs to the disseminating agency with minimum delay.

It is recommended that certain ground photo units be assigned to the major air force commands to provide public relations photography.

2. Availiability of Information of an Operational Nature to PRO Section

The Ninth Air Force endeavored to make all operational information, compatible with security, available to its public relations section, since it was felt that the section could function efficiently and produce outstanding and accurate news coverage only when it knew the complete tactical situation.

It is recommended that the air force policy on the availability of information to the PRO section be as liberal as possible without compromising the security of planning or disposition of forces. It is further recommended that the PRO officer or his delegated representative be required to attend such operational meetings as are necessary to enable him to maintain a continuous picture of the immediate situation and future operational plans to the same extent as a wing commander or group commander.

3. Press Camps

After considerable experimentation, the Ninth Air Force discovered that press camps could be most efficiently operated under a self-sustaining basis with their own arrangements for mess, transport, transport maintenance, communications, censorship, briefing and photography.

It is recommended that press camps wherever possible be operated on a self-sustaining basis, with their own living, housing and transport facilities.

K. FINANCE (Special Staff)

1. Finance Column in Command Headquarters T/O

Air force experience indicated the advisability of including in the tactical command headquarters T/O a finance column similar to that in the T/O of a standard air service group. Such a finance unit would be able to handle any administrative fiscal work for the command, in addition to paying command headquarters personnel. A static finance service was considered essential in so large an organization as a tactical command headquarters. In the Ninth Air Force such service was maintained by placing Ninth Air Force Finance Detachment at Large personnel on indefinite detached service at command headquarters. Although, for obvious administrative reasons, this method was far from satisfactory, it proved to be the only successful operating method of those tried.

It is recommended that a finance column be added to the T/Os of tactical commands.

L. MEDICAL (Special Staff)

1. Effective Use of Medical Dispensaries (Avn)

Various command and administrative problems which arose from having dispensaries operating with the tactical groups might have been solved by divorcing the medical dispensaries from tactical groups. There is no need, under the present authorization of air base group aid equipment, to have the dispensaries closely allied to the tactical groups. Satisfactory use of the dispensaries could be achieved by controlling them at command level and by placing them centrally in concentrations of air force units not on airfields (for instance, engineer battalions engaged in building "clutches" of airfields), in large headquarters areas or in centers of AAA brigade concentrations.

It is recommended that the principles for the employment of medical dispensaries (Avn) outlined above be considered as a basis for their future employment with tactical air forces.

2. Expeditious Movement of Hospitals

Maximum use of air force hospitals by air force units prevents unnecessary loss of time in the return of recuperated patients to duty. To achieve maximum use of such hospitals, it is necessary and justifiable to establish fairly high priority for the prompt movement of hospitals into the centers of air force population.

It is recommended that field hospital platoons be assigned to an air force headquarters and be completely at the disposal of that headquarters, so that expeditious movement of hospitals can be accomplished.

3. Simplification of Medical Reports

Much can be done to simplify medical reports. Elimination of certain reports, consolidation of information and speeding of the reporting routine would be helpful. It is believed that a true statistical evaluation of the medical situation in a command is possible under a greatly simplified reporting procedure.

It is recommended that an analysis be made of medical reports in general, with a view to simplifying reports and reducing their number.

4. Rotation of Medical Officer to Hospitals

Most medical officers deplore the lack of opportunity to practice medicine. An opportunity for occasional periods of duty in hospitals on an exchange basis would undoubtedly improve their morale. This was accomplished only to a very limited extent in the Ninth Air Force. Expansion of this exchange system to include duty in general hospitals would be desirable, but the operational aspects of such a plan present great difficulties.

It is recommended that every possible effort be made to work out an air force system of assigning all medical officers to a periodic tour of duty in hospitals.

5. Promotion of Medical and Dental Officers

A low state of morale existed among medical and dental-officers because of their comparatively low rank and the severe limitations of T/Os.

It is recommended that the professional services of medical and dental officers be recognized by authorizing increased rank.

BIBLIOGRAPHY

THIS REPORT is based upon: (a) repeated interviews with the key commanders and staff officers of all echelons of command of the Ninth Air Force, (b) detailed study and research submitted in report form from Headquarters Ninth Air Force and its command echelons and (c) a complete survey of the battle experience of and operating procedures developed not only by the Ninth Air Force and its commands but by all agencies with which the Ninth Air Force maintained operational and administrative liaison. USSTAF and 12th Army Group afforded the fullest cooperation, both by personal interview and by making the necessary material available for study and research to members of the publishing staff.

The following list comprises the more important reports and reference matter:

1. The Air Force in Theaters of Operation, May 1943.
2. FM 1–10, Air Corps Field Manual.
3. FM 31–35, Aviation in Support of Ground Forces, 9 April 1942.
4. FM 100–20, Command and Employment of Air Power.
5. "Effect of Air Power on Military Operations, Western Europe," by Air Effects Committee, 12th Army Group.
6. Ninth Air Force Periodic Staff Reports.
7. IX Tactical Air Command History.
8. XIX Tactical Air Command History.
9. XXIX Tactical Air Command History.
10. IX Troop Carrier Command History.
11. IX Air Defense Command History.
12. IX Engineer Command History.
13. IX Air Force Service Command History.
14. Ninth Air Force Historical Section Reports.
15. "12,000 Fighter Bomber Sorties," XIX Tactical Air Command.
16. G–2 Air Section Reports, 12th Army Group.
17. G–3 Air Section Reports, 12th Army Group.

18. Army Air Force Evaluation Board Report of Ninth Air Force Operations.
19. Statistical Summary of Ninth Air Force Operations.
20. "Reconnaissance in a Tactical Air Command," XIX Tactical Air Command.
21. Weekly Intelligence Summary of Operations, Ninth Air Force.
22. Invasion Activities Report, April through June 1944, Ninth Air Force.
23. Ninth Air Force Tactical Air Plan for "OVERLORD."
24. "Tactical Air Operations in Europe," XIX Tactical Air Command.
25. A Report on the Combat Operations of the XIX Tactical Air Command.
26. SOP's of Ninth Air Force and Commands.
27. SOI's of Ninth Air Force and Commands.

ABBREVIATIONS

AAA	—Antiaircraft Artillery.
AADA	—Advanced Air Depot Area.
A/C	—Aircraft.
A C/S	—Assistant Chief of Staff.
A/D	—Airdrome.
ADC	—Air Defense Command.
ADGB	—Air Defense of Great Britain.
ADSEC	—Advanced Section.
AEAF	—Allied Expeditionary Air Force.
AFSC	—Air Force Service Command.
AGCO	—Air-Ground Cooperation Officer.
AGRAB	—Army Group Rear Area Boundary.
AI	—Airborne Interception.
AIBR	—Acceleration Integrator Bombsight Release.
ALG	—Advanced Landing Ground.
ALO	—Air Liaison Officer.
APID	—Army Photo Interpretation Detachment.
A/R	—Armed Reconnaissance.
Arty/R	—Artillery Reconnaissance.
ASC	—Air Support Command.
BACU	—Battle Area Control Unit.
BADA	—Base Air Depot Area.
BDA	—Bomb Damage Assessment.
BUCO	—Build-Up Control Office.
CATOR	—Combined Air Transport Operations Room.
CG	—Commanding General.
COSSAC	—Chiefs of Staff, Supreme Allied Command.
CP	—Command Post.
CPX	—Command Post Exercise.
C/S	—Call Signal; Chief of Staff.
CWS	—Chemical Warfare Service.
CZ	—Communications Zone.
DCG	—Deputy Commanding General.
D C/S	—Deputy Chief of Staff.
DIO	—Duty Intelligence Officer.
E/A	—Enemy Aircraft.
ETO	—European Theater of Operations.
ETOUSA	—European Theater of Operations, United States Army.
FAAA	—First Allied Airborne Army.

FCC —Fighter Control Center.
FDP —Forward Director Post.
FM —Frequency Modulation.
FUSA —First United States Army.
FUSAG —1st United States Army Group.
GAF —German Air Force.
GCC —Group Control Center.
GCI —Ground Control Interception.
GEE —Radar Navigational and Blind Bombing Aid.
GLO —Ground Liaison Officer.
GP —General Purpose.
HF —High Frequency.
HVAR —High Velocity Aerial Rocket.
IAZ —Inner Artillery Zone.
IFF —Identification: Friend or Foe.
MAAF —Mediterranean Army Air Forces.
MEW —Microwave Early Warning.
MIS —Military Intelligence Service.
MLO —Movement Liaison Officer.
MOS —Military Occupational Specialty.
MT —Motor Transport.
M/Y —Marshalling Yard.
OBOE —Radar Blind Bombing Aid.
OEL —Organizational Equipment List.
OSS —Office of Strategic Services.
PAP —Pierced Aluminum Plank.
PHS —Prepared Hessian Surfacing.
PID —Photo Interpretation Detachment.
POL —Petroleum, Oil, Lubricants.
P/R —Photo Reconnaissance.
PRO —Public Relations Officer.
PROV —Provisional.
PSP —Pierced Steel Plank.
RCD —Reinforcement Control Depot.
RCM —Radio Counter Measures.
Recce —Reconnaissance.
R/T —Radio Telephone.
SAW —Signal Aircraft Warning.
SCR —Signal Corps Radio.
SCU —Statistical Control Unit.
Second TAF—Second Tactical Air Force (RAF).
SHAEF —Supreme Headquarters Allied Expeditionary Forces.
SHORAN —Radar Navigational and Blind Bombing Aid.

SIGABA SIGGUM SIGJIP SIGRINO SIGTOT	—Classified Cryptographic Equipment.
SMT	—Square Mesh Tracking.
SOI	—Standing Operating Instructions.
SOP	—Standing Operating Procedure.
SOS	—Services of Supply.
SSN	—Specialty Serial Number.
TAC	—Tactical Air Command.
TAC/R	—Tactical Reconnaissance.
TAD	—Tactical Air Depot.
TAF	—Tactical Air Force.
TALO	—Tactical Air Liaison Officer.
TCC	—Tactical Control Center.
T/E	—Table of Equipment.
T/O & E	—Tables of Organization and Equipment.
TOT	—Time Over Target.
TUSA	—Third United States Army.
TWX	—Teletype Message.
UK	—United Kingdom.
USAFI	—United States Armed Forces Institute.
USSAFUK	—United States Strategic Air Forces in the United Kingdom.
USSTAF	—United States Strategic Air Forces in Europe.
VHF	—Very High Frequency.
W/T	—Wireless Telegraphy.
X-Ray	—Code name for "X"; used for Advanced Party, and also for an unidentified track on a radar scope.
Y-Service	—Radio Intelligence Intercept.
ZI	—Zone of the Interior.